<u>LEGACY</u>

R. C. SEELY

THE WISE MAN IS A THREAT TO THE STATE, BUT THE IDEALIST NOT AFRAID TO DIE TO PROTECT HIS RIGHTS, COULD DESTROY THE STATE.

LEGACY

DEDICATED TO THOSE WHO LIVE IN, OR HAVE LIVED IN, TOTALITARIAN STATES. IN LOVING MEMORY OF THOSE WHO NEVER GOT OUT.

MAY YOUR WORST NIGHTMARES EVOLVE INTO YOUR BEST DREAMS.

PROLOGUE

"Did you get it?"

"Yes, Charles, everything you requested he was able to track down. Where did
you get the watch?

"Never mind." Charles replies.

"Come on. Tell me I want to know."

"If you must know. I got it off of
Albert.. After he passed."

"What! My God, have you lost your
mind? What if *they* had caught you?"

"*They* had more to deal with that day,
than one of *us* snatching a corpse's watch."

"That depends on which one you deal
with and their mood. You know that."

Charles sighs and hides his prizes
under his bed. "It was important."

"Important? You were risking your
life for a pencil and a piece of parchment.
Excuse my ignorance, but I don't see how
that was worth it."

"How old are you? Twenty-five,
twenty-six? At the most thirty. Were you
even married, before all this? I'm seventy-
eight. I've lived my life, I've had my adven-
tures. Traveled to Spain, England and

France. Had my children, seen them have their children. Seen the fruits of my labor get turned to dust, but those vile sons-of-"

Putting his head in his hands, the old man can't finish that statement. It takes a few moments but when he does lift his head back up his eyes are puffy and his face damp.

"I'm just glad Helena wasn't still with us to see our precious fatherland in the hands of these madmen. It sickens me to think that my fellow Germans fell for that Hitler's speeches. That's why I'm doing this. To make sure others after we're all gone remember what happened to us. That's what all this is about anyway, being immortalized. Being remembered, a Legacy. That's what the Fuhrer thinks is important at least. Not country, not family, just this twisted legacy.

I don't even know if my children are still alive. I hope so… That they escaped this mess. That the are not in one of these camps…"

He goes silent for a moment. "Have you ever read the works of Dante? The Divine Comedy, or The Inferno? I don't even fear the possibilities of it.. The torments of the Damned, don't scare me anymore. Not after this.. Not anymore.."

Then he turns his head, like it was a magnet being drawn to the opposing pole.

"Not again." The rest of the camp inhabitants notice it as well, some turn their heads to it, while others shy away. It's the smell. That horrible smell from the smokestacks. Some of the younger more curious detainees go to the window. When the full picture comes into view and it comes from the sky. To the casual observer it looks like snow but it's too heavy to be snow. Rather than washing all it touches clean, it stains everything. All that, and the smell, that horrible smell. That almost haunting aroma, that will bring back agony in their old age, at least the ones that make it to old age. Charles leans down, grabs the parchment and pencil. Using his bed as a writing desk, he starts writing.

I don't know what to expect while living here. To compare this to hell, is the closest I can think of to call it. I'm not sure that I will survive the night or if this is my last one. Not that this a foreign feeling anymore. At times I don't know that death would be so bad. Death.. The great sleep...

If I do live through this I don't

know where I will go or what I will do. The past few years have been nothing but death and destruction. I dare not hope, because at this point I feel that to be the only thing I have left they could take away from me. I don't know that I could bear that. So many people are dead. So many men. So many women. So many children. Innocent people who didn't do anything wrong.

I saw an old woman whose only crime was she spilled a bucket of water. It wasn't even her fault, when she spilled it. The SS officer shoved her. His superior saw the mess and started beating her. When he got tired of that, he pulled out his luger and finished the job. Her son, Hans, wasn't there when it happened but when he showed up I thought he was going to kill each and every officer there. He's young, maybe thirty at most. I asked a couple of the others to help hold him back and told him we wouldn't let him go until he calmed down. He resisted for awhile but then gave up when we were making good on that promise.

I sat with him while he cried on my

shoulder. We got to talking, I listened while he told of his mother and how great a woman she was. She was the salt of the earth, would have done anything for any-body. It took an hour and half to get him completely calmed down, but afterwards we went to the location of her shooting. By this time she had been taken away and all that was left was a puddle of blood. The funny thing is, I'm not sure if I feel sorry for her, or envy her.

At first the Nazis were satisfied with simply humiliating us, but now they are won't stop until we are all dead. A couple of years ago they started with the death camps. The most notorious, Auschwitz; at least it's not as bad here as it is there. We have heard stories from the guards here, meant to break our spirits, about the hor-rors of that place. Especially tales of the vile doctor named, Josef Mengele. They tell of his experiments, injecting them with different chemicals, sewing people to-gether, unimaginable experiments with twins. He is obsessed with twins. But we are all his dolls, his living playthings.

Insects for him to rip the wings off of and leave to die, alone... Alone...

The Nazis call us "Untermenschen" or the inferior ones. Their actions toward us reflect this attitude. Will anyone help us from this? CAN anyone help us?

What's even worse, we let this happen. Our religious leaders told our people not to fight back. What will the world think of us? What will our children think of us?

He puts the papers back in their hiding place between the bed and mattress. He climbs into bed and covers himself with the blanket, shielding himself from this warped reality.

CHAPTER 1

"Charlie.. Wake up!" says a female voice, from the other side of the door.

"What?.." comes the groggy and disoriented answer.

"Charles Thayer- Get out of bed right now! You don't want to be late for school!"

"Mmmm…" the thirteen year old replies, before pulling the covers over his head. The door opens and the next sensation is the sudden appearance of light, that comes from the intruder's ripping the top sheet that the child was using as a defense.

"Mom!" Charlie, says in protest.

"Don't 'Mom' me. Today's a big day, you know that. You have to take your Occupational Examines, it will change your whole life."

In further response she grabs her son by the collar of his shirt. "Your dad had to pull a lot of strings to get you in early to take these exams. Now get cleaned up."

"Alright, alright," Charlie mumbles in defeat, as he heads into the bathroom. He performs his normal morning tasks, brushing his teeth and showering.

He heads downstairs for breakfast.

"Did dad leave yet?"

"Yes, he had an early meeting at the senate. He said to wish you good luck with the examinations though."

"I hope that my results are to be a Senator like dad. Having the ability to change peoples lives like that. That would be so cool."

He hears the dishes that his mom was putting in the cabinet crash to the floor, but she's just grasping her forehead and not cleaning it up. She seems to be a trance almost, one of the shards of porcelain chipped on the counter before hitting the tile. As she steadies herself with her free hand she positions herself hand over it, cutting her hand. "Ahh.." She whimpers, more out of alarm than pain.

"Mom, are you okay?" Charlie asks, noticing for the first time her odd behavior.

"Yes, I'm fine. It's a just little cut.." Then she notices the plates in shatters. "I better get this cleaned up." She leaves the room; while gone Charlie keeps looking at the broken dishes. When she comes back she has the robotic broom following her. She also has a layer of liquid skin covering her wound. The laser on the robot finds the remains of the dishes, and a door on the front of the machine lowers. The broom darts out and like some kind of animal catching it's food with it's tongue, grabs the dishes and pulls them into the gaping mouth. It continues this until all the debris is collected. By this time the bored Charlie has already turned back to his cereal.

"You know, Charlie there are a lot of other worthwhile occupations out there. Engineers, or architecture, or something like that. Ones where you build things, those are very honorable and honest work."

Charlie sits there for a minute considering his mother's last statement. "Don't you think that dad is a man of honor or truth?" he finally asks her.

"Yes, of course I do sweetie. More now than ever," she replies.

Another perplexing comment from his mother, but he doesn't have time to fixate on it.

"Hurry and get ready we have to get you to the Occupational Examinations Department Office, and it's across town."

He finishes the rest of his cereal and puts his dishes in the sink, grabs his coat and they head to the car.

They place their hands on the their car doors, over a pad on the door. The pad lights up and a green band at the top of the pad appears and slides down to the bottom of the pad. The pad lights up green and the door pops open. When inside the vehicle the safety strap slides across them and locks into place. A voice from the car comes prompts a question. DESTINATION, it asks. "Occupational Examinations Department Office," Mrs. Thayer says in a clear distinct voice.

DESTINATION AFFIRMED-OCCUPA-TIONAL EXAMINATIONS DEPARTMENT OFFICE-TIME REQUIRED THIRTY FIVE MINUTES, the car replies.

The car then starts up and turns on a music selection from the government approved satellite radio. About fifteen minutes into the broadcast, the music is interrupted by a news brief. "The Overlord has just signed a law that will extend the curfew ten minutes, to ten-ten. Yesterday, a group of revolutionaries in the area near the Capital building have been caught and tried by our Justice Department for crimes of treason against the Overlord. Their executions will be carried out today at five in the afternoon, all citizens are encouraged to attend.

The meal served to attendees shall be Montreal Steak and Baked Sweet Potatoes, with a White Chardonnay.

In other news, Mrs. Hamilton had this to say about our benevolent Overlord "Oh, How great our Overlord is. If not for him my husband would have to figure out his own job and would waste all that valuable working time on trying to figure that out. What a hassle that would have been. So thank you Overlord Tymes." Now back to your government music station. Long live Overlord Tymes."

Mrs. Thayer has been staring out the window during the news brief, making sure her son didn't see the tear running down her cheek. She wipes it away before turning to him a broad smile on her pretty face and she tussles his hair.

The rest of the ride is in an unusual silence, Mrs. Thayer is a very chatty woman especially with her family and when Charlie exits, his mom steps out of the car as well. She hugs him and says just one thing. "I love you, Charlie. Just know that."
No good luck on the exams. No I'll see you at home. *I love you, Charlie. Just know that*, following a long and hard hug. One more very odd incident, to this very odd day. Mrs. Thayer gets back into the car a waves good-bye to her son and then turns her head staring out the window again.

Charlie watches her leave for a couple of minutes perplexed by what has transpired to-day and turns to enter the government building.

Charlie has never been in this building before and follows the gentle guide force of the automatic doors. In the enormous lobby are holographic, moving pictures of all five of the Overlords. Showing video clips of them at their greatest triumphs. Past the statues and columns, at the back of the spacious lobby is a large desk with elevators, five on each side, and sitting at the desk is a spindly unimposing man. On each side of him are a couple of very massive and imposing armed guards. On their sides in holsters are tasers. He steps up behind the next person in the line of five or six people. Each person is being searched before redirected to their elevator, where a single operator is inside. It's only the operator and a single rider occupying the elevators at any time, this is a security measure for government buildings decried by the third Overlord in his first year.

A couple of hours later, it's Charlie's turn, one of the guards pats him down and the other searches his bag as is common procedure.

Then the man behind the desk asks him to approach, he has Charlie turn around and pulls a device from his desk. It's a plain looking scanner like one found at a grocery store. He points it at Charlie's neck, at the barcode that is tattooed on the back of the child's neck specifically. He scans the mark and on the holographic screen he pulls up all the information on the boy. The holographic screen has a series of menus; *Medical History, Financial History, Educational History and Grades, Family History and Genetics* and *Occupational History*.

With a shaking hand, the man behind the desk touchs the *Occupational History* menu. He reads the only entry, Charles Thayer here for Occupational Examination. The man at the desk then gestures for the guard to come close and whispers something in his ear. In a booming voice the guard tells Charlie, "Elevator Six," and points to the elevator Charlie is supposed to go to. "Thank you," Charlie says and enters the elevator. The door to it opens and he sees the elevator operator up close. He's in a plain suit and tie, with a name badge that reads Harold. "Hi Harold, I'm Charlie," Charlie says in the innocence common to children.

"Hi Charlie," Harold replies less cordially.

"Do you like your job?" Charlie asks.

"Yes, I do," Harold responds, not very convincingly.

"I'm sorry. Did I do something wrong? Or do you not like children?" Charlie asks.

"No.. We are just not supposed to talk, just operate the elevator," Harold answers back.

"It's an efficiency thing, they say."

"Oh, I didn't know. I'm sorry. I don't mean to get you into trouble. I'm kind of nervous about the exams, I guess." Harold smiles.

"It's okay. I'm sure you'll do well."

"Thank you," Charlie says.

It's a short ride up to the Examinations floor and Charlie stands there looking around the room. He then swallows and enters. "Good luck, Charlie. This is a day of fate for you."

Charlie turns back, but before he can say anything the elevator doors close. For a minute Charlie stands there, then he turns and shakes his head. He heads up to the counter and is greeted by a cheery young woman.

"How may I help you?" she asks, in a high voice that almost hurts the ears.

"Yes, I'm here to take my Occupational Examinations," Charlie states.

"Okay, well I have to have you sign in first off," she says while handing him an electronic clipboard. He signs on the line and the signature disappears and the clipboard reads; `Signature Match Confirmed- Charles Thayer.`   Charlie hands the clipboard back to the woman.

"Alright then, come with me and we will get you going with the examination." She leads Charlie to a series of lockers and scans the back of his head. She then places his thumb on one of the lockers and it opens up.

"We need you to place all you belongings, your bag, keys, anything in your pockets, in the locker, before preceding to the examination room. When you're done with the exam, to get your belongings back put your thumb on the thumb-plate and the lock will disengage. Good luck and have a good day." She walks away and he realizes why she was so bubbly, that gait isn't human. She's a android. A 'Help-Bot' of some kind.

He places his belongings in the locker hearing the whirl and click of the camera behind and above him. Monitoring every motion, it moves when he moves, Charlie has never really felt comfortable with all the cameras. But it was a call that was not his to make So he now heads to the examination room for the examination. He sits down at the assigned cubicle and waits to be told he can begin. At another cubicle, its inhabitant gets started without permission and immediately a man in a suit comes up and takes the boy out of the room. Seeing this, Charlie sits waiting for the indication that he can start. He gets it, opens his booklet and puts on his headset. A mechanical voice comes on and commands his attention.

///Hello Charles, Welcome to the Occupational Examinations 3000 Series. The first part of the Examination will be simple multiple choice questions. After that will be a series of True or False. Followed by Range of Motion, Natural Abilities and an Intelligence and Emotional Abilities Evaluations. Ending in an Essay Question about what occupation you want and why. Are you ready to begin??//

Charlie says, "Yes." ///The Examinations begin Now..///

Charlie goes through the examination, answering every question. After the first couple of hours they are given a half hour break. Charlie heads into the bathroom. This is where his real brush with fate is to occur.

He heads to the locker to get his bag, then

goes to the restroom. Before going in a guard is seen running around frantic.

"Did you seen a dirty, dark-haired child anywhere?" he asks Charlie. Charlie shakes his head. He watches the guard run off again and enters the restroom. He heads into one of the rooms putting his open bag on the floor. Preoccupied with the events of the days he doesn't even notice the small hand reaching underneath the gap between the stalls. But the owner of the hand isn't taking anything, but instead is placing a book in Charlie's bag. He's shaken from his train of thought by the sounds of someone running from the next stall and out of the room.

"HELLO?" Charlie calls out. Wow! What a weird day," Charlie says aloud.

Charlie heads back to finish his examinations.

When he gets done with the examinations than he goes through the security checkpoints unmolested, mostly because there was a unruly man in the lobby when he was leaving so the guards were focused on him instead. If they had examined the contents of his bag more closely, that might not have been the case.

CHAPTER 2

"So how did the examinations go?" Mrs. Thayer, asks her son as he climbs into the car.

"Fine," Charlie answers, with a note of reluctance in his voice.

"You don't sound too sure Charlie. What's wrong?"

"It has nothing to do with the examina tions. There were just some weird things that happened while there," he replies.

"Oh? Like what?" she asks. Charlie tells her about the elevator operator and the incident with the guard and the child.

"It's just been a strange day all the way around."

"We all get that feeling every now and then," Mrs. Thayer answers back.

"I guess," Charlie says. Mrs. Thayer hugs her son.

"We had better hurry we don't want to be late," Mr. Thayer tells his wife and Charlie.

"Yes because it's not everyday there's an execution," Mrs. Thayer snidely replies.

"Stop it Evelyn! Just because I'm a Sen- ator and the house isn't wired, doesn't mean we can let our guard down and make remarks like that," Mr. Thayer snaps back, in an angry whisper to his wife.

"We have to think about Charlie and make sure everything seems normal, at least until Robert can get him."

"I still don't know about all this, I mean how do we know your brother is right about all this? Robert was always a little out there and now we are risking everything for this," Mrs. Thayer asks.

Mr. Thayer holds his wife's hands and rests his forehead on her forehead.

"I can't live with what I have allowed to happen. I can't ignore my part in it. Knowing that my actions were really helping to hurt those who put such faith in me. Can you honestly tell me that this isn't right?"

"I don't know what to think anymore…" Mrs. Thayer trails off. "I just want to hurry and get this night over with."

"I know. So do I," he says, as they fall into each other's arms.

"Are you two ready yet?" Charlie says, while standing at the door.

"Yes," Mrs. Thayer says, smiling while still looking at her husband. Than she turns to Charlie and straightens his tie. She gently caresses his cheek. "My only child. You are so grown up."

The executions are like the other ones, they start out with the usual fanfare. The celebrities and dignitaries that show up are asked for an interview. The most asked questions being about their next enterprise, or what designer clothing they are wearing. Nothing about their feelings, concerning the reason for this gathering. Then come the Senators and their families. Mr. Thayer is stopped and asked questions, about some law that he signed, Mrs. Thayer is asked if she's proud of her husband and his work.

"I've always been proud of my husband and I only get more so everyday I get to spend with him. I couldn't be any luckier," she responds, rubbing her husband's arm. Finally done with the mandatory pleasantries of a Senator's family, Charlie and his parents are shown to their seats. As the crowd settles down, a man in a suit steps up to the pulpit and leans into the microphone.

"Ladies and gentlemen, boys and girls, we are gathered here today to see a group of cowardly rebels receive justice. They have plotted to usurp our society and plunge it into utter chaos. Ours is one of order, conformity and unity. We cannot tolerate such actions of distinctiveness from the status quo. Such reckless abandonment of uniformity is dangerous to us all. You and I know that our great Overlord will protect us, but only if we are as one. That is why such actions against the Overlord can't go unpunished. LONG LIVE OVERLORD TYMES!" the announcer almost screams the last words.

"LONG LIVE OVERLORD TYMES!" the crowd answers back.

"So we will now start the ceremony, with the singing of our National Anthem, then the executions and finish with a fireworks display during dinner." With that the announcer steps away from the pulpit and a spot light is positioned on the gallows where a microphone has been placed. A girl probably seven or eight years old, steps out of the shadow and up to the microphone. In a surprisingly strong voice, the little child sings the song in very mellifluous tones. After the anthem and she has left the stage, five spot lights appear on the gallows for the condemned. Then another spotlight goes to the side of the arena, where the first man is brought out. On his garment is a single word; TRAITOR. The guard that is right behind him forces him to the first noose and takes his place behind the prisoner. Another prisoner steps out with his shadow guard accompanying him and this continues until all the prisoners are out; two men, two women, and one twelve year old child with dark matted hair. Charlie recognizes one of them as the man who created the ruckus in the Government Office. All of them are dirty and look like they are from the outskirts of the Capitol City. The guards step up to place the nooses around the necks of the condemned. In a uniform procession, the guards exit the stage.

A band off to the sidelines, in the shadows starts the 'execution ballad', with the child who sang the anthem singing with them in chorus.

A man in military uniform with a sword at his side steps on the stage. He pulls out the sword. He holds it out in the air up above his head and in one swipe cuts through the air, forcing the tip to the floor. That's the signal for the trap doors to open. What was once floor under the prisoners feet is now open space. Only one of the women is lucky enough to have her neck break instantly. The rope on one of the men has ripped his neck open and sliced the jugular vein, causing him to bleed out on the stage. As for the rest they will strangle. The boy is the first to stop struggling. Then the woman, and the last is the man left to bleed to death.

During the last few minutes of their lives the band ends the 'execution ballad' with the drums imitating the beating of a human heart. Slowing as the condemned breath their last gasp of air. As it ends silence fills the room. Then exuberant cheers from the audience fills the arena. Tears of joy flow from the crowd. The most notable exception to this is Mr. and Mrs. Thayer, both putting on the mask of joy but in truth feeling heartbroken at the sight. As the guards take the bodies away, the crowd gets inspired and break into a little ditty.

"LONG LIVE OVERLORD TYMES, LONG LIVE OVERLORD TYMES, DEATH

TO ALL TRAITORS, DEATH TO ALL TRA-
ITORS," says the   crowd over and over. As the
impromptu song praising the Overlord continues,
the harder Mrs. Thayer's grip on her husband's
hand gets, until they feel pins and needles, and
has to let go.

With all the fuss done, the Thayers can
finally relax and enjoy their meals. They watch
the fireworks with a sudden sense of calm at
last.

Then that feeling of uneasiness comes
back when the fireworks end and the highlights
of past executions is shown on the gigantic tele-
vision screens. One of the hangings that affects
them the most is the botched one that ended in a
beheading. The rope popped the head off and a
trail of red followed the body as it fell to the
ground, ending in a pool under the headless man.
Then it gets worse and starts showing footage
from the early days of the executions when they
were still searching for the most ideal method-
ology.

Burning at the stakes, hearing the condemned screaming and the foul smell it was abandoned. Lethal injection, not gruesome enough.
Beheading and disembowelings, these were excellent crowd-pleasers and are still used for
single prisoner executions or senators and dignitaries, but impractical for multiple executions.
With all the tried ways to kill, hangings would
end up being the most efficient.

Mrs. Thayer takes a large sip of her wine at the end of the show.

The ride home is a quiet one, as the family reflects on the sights and sounds of the evening. Charlie adds all that to the odd events early this day. On the car's radio comes the news break.

"The executions of the convicted traitors went smoothly and the bodies have been hung from the Center Bridge, where they will stay for the next three days until taken down and incinerated. It was a routine execution without any incidents. That's the end of our broadcast today, we will have more news tomorrow starting at six am. Thank you. Long live Overlord Tymes."

Mr. and Mrs. Thayer look at each other and he kisses her hand. As they pass under the bridge Charlie sees the remains of the five condemned, all with lights on them and still wearing the garments that read; TRAITOR. Only now they look less human after being embalmed for preservation. The sight makes Charlie shudder.

When the get home the family finds a visitor out in their driveway. "Uncle Robert," Charlie says jubilantly as he runs up to the grey haired, scruffy man.

"Hey kiddo. How's my superstar?" he greets his nephew.

"I'm good. We just got back from the executions, did you go to them? We didn't see you there."

"No, I couldn't I had work to do," he replies.

"Work? No one works during the executions. It's a mandatory time off," Charlie asks.

"Nothing gets by you. So how'd your
Occupational Examinations go?" Robert asks.

"We'll get the results in a couple of
weeks," Charlie answers.

"That long, huh," Robert replies.

"Come on in, Charlie. It's getting cold,"
Mrs. Thayer says.

"Okay."

"Hey, Bobby. How are you?" Mr. Thayer
asks his older brother.

"Better now that I've seen you folks,"
Robert responds.

"Coming in for a drink?" Mr. Thayer asks.

"Sounds good to me."

"I could use one," Mrs. Thayer whispers,
as she enters their home.

The sound of clinking ice cubes in glass is
the only sound in the house. Charlie has gone
upstairs. It's only the three adults in the room.

"So how did it go?" Robert asks.

"I don't know," Mr. Thayer answers back.
 "Charlie hasn't said anything about it. He mentioned the disturbance at the Government Office
building, but not about the book itself."

"Robert, are you sure about this? Can
you really protect our son?" Mrs. Thayer interrupts.

"No, I can't, but my associates can. I

understand your concerns, but this is not their first time doing this. They have gotten many refugees across the border and once they claim asylum status they can't be touched," Robert answers.

While his parents and Robert talk Charlie goes through his stuff in his bag. Looking for his videogame system to play with before bed. Instead he comes across something that he didn't even know was in there, a very rudimentary book. It's very old and the binding is falling apart. In a fading embossed silver, the title is the only thing clear to the eyes, it reads only a single word; LEGACY. Charlie checks the window, the shades are closed. He checks the door, the adults are still down stairs. He opens the book. Nowhere does it say who wrote it. On the title page is the same single word; LEGACY. There's no copy rite page, no publishing information.

Not that it would still be viable, since the first Overlord abolished all property rights and the third Overlord outlawed a selection of books that proved contrary to his philosophy. Even if it did have the copy rite Charlie wouldn't know what it was.

Charlie reads the first page,
There will always be tyranny somewhere, of some kind. It's a part of the human condition, as is a gift of great Charity. The worse of these tyrants will claim neither exists, to kill all

source of possible hope. When a culture has reached that point, then and only then, is its fate of destruction inevitable.

When it has reached that point than its people know not a different society, and if it knows not of any other possibilities to dream of. That is why all is lost.

Charlie reads the first page over considering it before turning to the next page.

Chapter 1

I don't know who, if anyone will ever read this. I'm sure I will be long dead before that point, but I have to do my part to make sure the future is not repeated. This all started when I found the manuscript. I don't know who wrote it. It had just the single word written on it- LEGACY. I will not take credit for those segments of this book. In the list of possible philosophers who could have wrote it are; Plato, Aristotle, Leonardo Di Vinci, Thomas Moore or Machiavelli. I found it in Paris, France right before Adolf Hitler and the Nazi's took control of our Germany.

After reading the book I understood what signs to look for to avoid their regime of enslavement, death, and eventual destruction. I

*wrote copies of it to my family, so they could
evacuate our country. Being Jewish, this was
more than just a pressing desire, but also a
very survival instinct. They did not heed my
warnings. To whomever reads this watch for
the signs and DO NOT IGNORE THEM.*

*If the signs had been acknowledged,
Atlantis might have been saved, Rome might
not have been burned, Greece may not have
fallen, and the Third Reich might never have
existed.*

From, the found manuscript;
"Law 1 for the Tyrant:
*The first thing to look for is a man of
false promises. If he promises world peace he is
not to be trusted, for he knows he cannot fulfill
 this claim. Not without the destruction of all
organic beings. Not only the human animal,
but all beings of any higher intellect. Man is
the most destructive of them, that cannot be
denied."*

*When the Fuhrer came to power that was
the promises he made. That he would save the
German people. We were in a deep depression
when Hitler was given the position of Chanc-*

ellor. He was our hero, our savior. What was not known by the masses was he would create more suffering. That the door to our own self-destruction would be flung wide open..

"Charlie," Robert says, as he enters the room.

"AHHH!" Charlie shouts, in surprise.

"Sorry, my boy I didn't mean to scare you," Robert says.

"It's okay I guess I was just getting into this book."

"What are you reading, Charlie?"

"I don't know I found it in my bag," Charlie answers back.

"Legacy.. Charlie, I wouldn't tell anyone about this book. It looks illegal," Robert instructs.

"Okay, I won't."

"Good lad. Anyway, I came up to say goodnight. I've got to go home and take care of some things. I love you pal."

"I love you too," Charlie says, and hugs his uncle.

Robert closes the door, watching his nephew immediately go back to the book.

"That's a good lad," Robert whispers outside the door.

Before getting outside the house Robert tells Mr. and Mrs. Thayer about his recent discovery. "Charlie has the book. The mission has been successful so far."

"Here's some of his things then. I packed a bag while he was gone," Mrs. Thayer says. "You promised to watch over him. Remember that."

"With my very life," Robert replies.

CHAPTER 3

It's early in the morning when a sound in-side his room wakes up the pacified Charlie. He's about to fall back to sleep, when a hand comes across his mouth. A man dressed in a military uniform is in his room huddles over him.

"SSSHHHH!" he says, with his finger in front of his lips. "Get up, you have to come with us," the stranger says. He gets up so Charlie can climb out of bed. That's when Charlie notices another figure behind the soldier.

"Get up now! You little.." the soldier do-esn't get to finish his statement, because the other man puts his hand other his mouth. Charlie sees a large blade exit the first stranger, and he feels the spray of hot, sticky blood hit his face and bed covers. The blade is pulled back out and the intruder drops like a rag doll.

"Charlie, get up. I have to get you out of here." This voice he recognizes, it's his uncle Robert. "Come on we have to go now."

Charlie climbs out of his no longer safe bed. "Grab the book," Robert instructs. Charlie grabs it. Robert bends down to talk to his nep-hew at eyelevel. "Hold tight to that book with that hand and to me with the other. Always look forward and do exactly what I say. Okay?"

"Okay," Charlie agrees.

They burst out of the bedroom and into the hallway, where more soldiers in uniform are in combat with a group of strangers, men and women, all in civilian clothes. Many are already covered in blood and other debris. A couple obviously dead, laying on the floor. Charlie catches a glance at the glossy lifeless eyes of the body turned his way, and holds his uncle's arm even tighter. As they push through the soldiers and exit through the front entry, Charlie sees his parents kneeling on the ground with arm restraints.

"Mom, Dad," he says and starts heading to them.

"Charlie, no. We can't help them. But I can make sure you're safe."

Robert forcefully pulls his reluctant nephew into a van around the corner.

"Let's go!" Robert tells the driver.

"What's happening? What's going on? Where are they taking my parents?" Charlie shouts frantically to no one in particular.

"Calm down, Charlie. I'll answer those questions as best I can once you calm yourself," Robert replies, hugging Charlie tightly, in part for both of their needs. As Charlie settles and the adrenaline rush fades, he vomits and then drifts off into unconciousness.

When he wakes and sits up, he finds himself greeted by the sun.

"What time is it?" Charlie asks. "Almost six, the first broadcast will be coming on soon," Robert replies. "Where are my parents?"

"The Overlord considers them to be enemies of the state. The Clergy got them."

"The Clergy? What's that?" Charlie asks.

"The Overlord's secret guards. They were the soldiers that broke into your home. The ones who were at the Government Office. They are people in your neighborhood. They use them because being your neighbors; those who come across them will be less likely to oppose them. They use your trust as a weapon against you."

"Are my parents dead?" Charlie asks, in a reluctant, very low whisper.

"I don't know, Charlie. I wish I did. For now just rest. We get you across the border, then we'll figure something out."

Charlie is almost asleep again, when he hears the first announcement. "Good Morning citizens. Last night, more traitors were found, including a prominent Senator and his wife. Their executions are planned for tomorrow afternoon. It has been delayed, because of the necessity of an extended inquisition. More news.."

Charlie doesn't hear the rest, the sounds just droning into white noise. He's too exhausted to even focus to comprehend it and at this point, he doesn't really care anymore.

While his nephew sleeps, Robert picks up the book, the one that his brother and his wife sacrificed their lives to keep safe. He starts reading it, until he sees the checkpoint comes into view. "Charlie, wake up."

"What is it?" Charlie asks groggily.

"We are almost at the first checkpoint."

"Uncle Rob, what about my RFID? They check that and they will know who I am."

"I've already got it covered. Your RFID barcode reads the information about you that is already in their file database. While you were asleep, I placed a strip over it that changed the information on it and it will give them the identity we created for you. Don't worry. We all are someone else, someone who really doesn't even exist."

"What about the book?"

"Also hidden, in plain sight. The checkpoint officers won't be looking for us for awhile and by then we will be across the border. That's all you need to know."

"So we are heading north?" Charlie asks.

"Yes, going through three checkpoint before the border," replies one of the other passengers in the van. "You're right Robert, this one definitively keeps a close eye on things."

"We need to go north to get out of the Overlord's reign, then we can come up with a real game plan," Robert says.

"We're at the checkpoint. So stick to

the script."

"What script?" Charlie asks.

Robert chuckles and then replies.

"Charlie, relax we have it covered. You trust me don't you?"

"Yes.." Charlie replies.

"Then, just enjoy the ride."

At the first checkpoint is about a dozen guards in all, checking the occupants of different vehicles. Charlie grabs his Uncle's arm with every foot closer to the border that they get. Charlie looks to the other seat and notices the book is sitting there, out in the open. His gaze doesn't leave it and he starts to shudder. Robert puts his arm around him and starts rubbing his back.

The van and its occupants have reached the border and the guard approaches the open window of the driver.

"How are you doing today? What is your purpose for leaving the country?" one of the guard asks. "We are just going on vacation. This is a couple of my friends and his nephew," the driver answers.

"Okay, I need to check your ID's. Hold out your arms," the guard instructs.

The men in the car do as told and the man waves the wand over the barcode tattoos.

"Everything checks out," he says. Then he comes to the back seat and Robert and Charlie. He sees Charlie shivering.

"What's wrong with him?" the man asks, in a tone that is full of cynicism, not concern.

"Nothing," Robert responds. "He's just a little carsick is all." The guard peeks in and notices the slight aroma of vomit and cleaner, and the dark stain on the carpet where Charlie's dinner remains once were. Satisfied the guard starts to walk off, Charlie sighs in relief and finally relaxes. But the flood of emotion rushes back in hurry, with the next statement out of the guard. "What's that on the seat?"

Charlie closes his eyes, trying disparately to make it go away. All of it.. His parents didn't get captured and by now maybe killed, and he's not here trying to cross the border for his life. He's at home in his nice warm bed, enjoying the reality that his life has been for the past twelve years. A couple of tears slide down his face as his new reality comes crashing down on him. The life he knew is gone and that no matter how badly he wishes all this away; this is his new life.

"So what is that?" the guard demands again.

"It's a book of antiquity. I got it from a licensed collector. If you need it I have the documentation for it," Robert says, and grabs a piece of paper from underneath the book and hands it to the guard. The guard studies the credentials before handing it back to him. He waves them through. Charlie still can't relax, in fact he starts to cry.

"I'm sorry, Charlie. I'm sorry for all of this.." Robert says, trying to soothe him.

"I know this is hard for you and I hope that someday you will understand the reasons why your parents did this. Understand it for what it is; a sacrifice. They want so very much for you, they have chosen to sacrifice their own lives for it."

Charlie falls asleep again, but after a couple of hours he wakes up hungry. "Do we have anything to eat?" he asks.

"Yeah.. We have sandwiches in the cooler," Robert answers, and hands him a sandwich. While eating his sandwich, Charlie watches the scenery passing his field of vision. This is the first time that he had been outside the Capitol city. He had heard about what it was like; rural communities, farmlands and industrial plants. He found out that was an outright lie. It's not the industrial haven that he was always told it was.

Instead, he sees dark bleak houses falling apart from abandonment and neglect. The inhabitants of this city look to match these surrounding. Dirty and malnourished, most of them are not more than walking skeletons. A child sits alone in the street staring at the travelers. A haunting expressionless look on her face. Void of the slightest true comprehension and curiosity, it reminds Charlie of the corpse on the floor in his house. Fires rage on, unchecked by anyone.

Soldiers goosestep in unified formation around the city. Searching out those supposed lawbreakers to be tried in a mock court. In an alley a couple of soldiers restrain and brutalize an unarmed and outnumbered civilian. Beating him and tasing him with their shock sticks, clubs with electrodes on the end. A boy, probably the man's son, runs from that same alley is tased with the prongs from the wireless tasers.

"What's happening to that boy?" Charlie asks. Robert looks up to follow Charlie's gaze.

"See that in the soldier's hand?" Charlie nods in response. "That's called a 'Taser.' It launches a projectile with a set of prongs that has a battery on it. The prongs sends an electrical current when it cuts into the skin. The first tasers had wires that sent the current, then someone designed a model that used a battery and projectile so it was more efficient."

"So, that boy is getting shocked? Why?" Charlie asks.

This time the answer comes from the man in the front seat. "They think they can make us do what they want if they show us what happens when we disobey them. But we know the laws better than they do and we figured out ways to circumvent their reign."

Charlie starts to mulls this over, when he notices the book again. He picks it up and runs his fingers over the cover. He opens it up and starts reading it again.

My mother died a couple of years before the war. After a five year battle with cancer, she received a merciful end and died in her sleep. My father, Charles, never recovered from this. After her death he had a long hard road of agony. When it first happened, he suffered from a bout of depression and even attempted suicide. Essentially when she died, he died. I always felt bad that I couldn't help him. We all did, all his family. We tried everything we could think of to restore his spirit, his will to live. Then it happened... The Nazi's started rounding us up. Things had literally changed overnight, yesterday we were everyday normal German citizens. Then we were vermin, in fact we were called vermin right to our faces. We were spit on. We were demonized by our neighbors. Our shops were ransacked. We were marked on our clothing with the Star of David, and so were our shops. This was the just the beginning.

The only thing that was good for our family, was the affect it had on dad. He came back to life when he saw how we were being treated. He didn't care what they did to him, he was worried about his family. He had come back from the dead.

As the war progressed so did the horrendous treatment the Jews would receive. First, *separating us from the rest of society. Then, encampment. Then, experimentation. Lastly, executions. The Jews were not the only ones to be treated this way though. Gypsies, homosexuals, Christians, anybody that was considered to be deviants of any kind from the 'Master Race' , were in the targets of the Nazi's. I didn't experience any of this, I left before it happened and left for the land of opportunity. It was a difficult and costly journey, even then the anti-Semitism that Hitler propagandized was already prevalent in the rest of Europe. Remember that the Nazi's didn't create this attitude, they just manipulated what was already there. I didn't find out the fate of the Jewish people, until later as I traveled postwar Europe for evidence of my family. I found writings from my father in one of the concentration camps, I found out later he wound up in Auschwitz a couple of weeks later. He was sent to the gas chambers shortly after. It was on his Eightieth birthday. My brothers had followed my lead and left, he died not ever knowing what had happened to his children.*

My search for artifacts took me into Italy. While there, I heard a tale of a book that would change my life. So I asked around, I asked priests, hotel owners, whoever I could find to give me a lead. It was, of all people, a shoeshine boy who gave me a real lead. His father has it. I was allowed to see the text, but he re-

fused to disclose how he came to possess it. I studied it for a couple of weeks and wrote down the most important segments of it, as well as those of my father's writings. After reading how it came together, legacy seemed like the only title choice for it. I hope this gets into the hands of those who would use it to further the cause of a free humanity.

" Law 2 for the Tyrant:

Another sure sign of the destructive nature in the heart of a leader, is in his childhood home. If he didn't grow up with a paternal figure, he will always be chasing a ghost. He will be wanting to emulate not a person, but the ideas of a person. But the end result will not be one of good fortune for him. What he is seeking is praise and adulation from the one who can't fulfill this need. He is doomed to a destiny of a hole; a deep, unyielding pit. That means he will never change course, no matter how inhumane or deplorable his actions and philosophies. Or if failure is clearly the results of his current path."

Charlie looks up from his book and turns to his uncle to ask him a question about it, when he notices a little smile on his scruffy face. It's something out the window that has Robert's attention fixed. Charlie moves closer to see. It's another interaction between a soldier and a civilian, but this one is unusual. The civilian is not on the ground in restraints, and his body posture is making it very clear he has absolutely no intention of complying with the instruction of doing so. He also is holding his right arm back out of sight of the officer. In response, the officer steps closer to the man, shock wand at the ready. But the odds change in the man's favor in a split second as he reveals what he was holding, a large knife about two feet long is extended at his aggressor. The officer starts backing up and places his hand on his taser. The man sees this and charges him like some kind of angry beast in musk. He knocks them both down and the man with the knife is the first to right himself. Kneeling on the soldier he starts stabbing him, over and over, until the soldier stops struggling. Breathing hard, the man looks like he is swimming in a red sea, soaked to the skin with the other man's blood. When he wipes his nose with his arm, the man notices the blood and panics. Dropping the knife, he runs inside his house and slams the door. Under the soldier, a pool of blood is already forming.

Charlie finds himself oddly titillated by the gruesome scene. Not by the sight itself, but by the greater context of the events. By the exchange of force. It's not a happy feeling exactly either, more of a feeling of satisfaction. It's very alien to him whatever it is.

"Uncle Rob, what just happened?" Charlie asks.

"That was resistance…" he replies. "That was hope." The man from the front seat looks back and smiles at both of them. He turns as something outside catches his eye. The trees are massive ones. They have left the city and entered the forests. They pull over to the side of the road and get out. This is the first time Charlie had been out in the natural world and he finds it beyond exhilarating. He closes his eyes so he can focus on all the smells and sounds. He bends down and grabs a handful of dirt in each hand and brings it up to his face. He takes in its unique aroma and breaks it up in his hands. He hears a bird far off in a distant tree. He sees a couple of squirrels fighting over some food.

The rumble of the ground and the sound of a motor wakes the group from the serenity of the forest. "Get back, Charlie. Hide in the trees," Robert instructs. Charlie nods and does just that. Charlie sees the men put their hands behind them, reaching under their shirts. As the sound gets louder, the men get more alert, then they suddenly relax. Charlie, not realizing that he had been holding his breath, lets out a huge sigh himself, seeing the rest of his party ease. The vehicle races up the road and all they see is a dark green blur. "You can come out now,

Charlie," Robert says.

"Was that who I think it was?" the driver asks the other men. "I think so," replies the other man. "Yeah, it was," Robert agrees. "The guy that killed that soldier is on the run. Hopefully he'll make the border, we can use as many resistance fighters as we can get."

"You guys are with the rebels??" Charlie asks, stunned.

"Yes Charlie, we are. So were your parents. You see, your father found out what was happening out here, outside of the Capitol City, and realized that we had inadvertently helped to enslave the very people he thought he was helping. Your father was a good man and only wanted to help, but he was misled.

Almost like destiny, I fell in with the rebels and got a hold of information that could help the resistance. That book we've been carrying is one of those pieces.

Out here, outside the Capitol City, things are very different. Perilous as the urban cities can be, they are nothing compared to the industrial areas. We call them the 'Graveyards' because that is all they are, places for people to die. Drones patrol the area, cameras and microphones are everywhere. For that man, who killed that officer, to even question a representative of the state was a death sentence... Of course, going with him would have been as well. This country has been killing itself for decades and the worst thing is, it's citizens let it happen."

"Let's go, Robert," the driver says.

"Come on, Charlie," Robert says, gently guiding his nephew back to the van.

The ride to the next checkpoint is in silence. At the next checkpoint Charlie sees something. "Look! It's that guy, he's trying to cross the border," Charlie exclaims.

"Let him pass. Let him pass," Robert says repeatedly, almost like a chant.

The group watches nervously, as his turn comes up. He gets stopped. He exits his vehicle, with soldiers' tasers fixed on him. Obviously, they know what he has done. For a moment Robert considers jumping out to help him, but Charlie grabs his arm and brings him back to reality. He has his own mission and that action would place it in jeopardy. So he stays put and they watch.

Noncompliant as ever the man reaches for the knife and again starts attacking soldiers. Anyone in a uniform gets his wrath and this time he's not alone. The two other men in the car jump out and come to his aid with their own equally large knives. A death sentence for even possessing. A swarm of soldiers leave their posts, waving everyone else through to join in. This is good fortune for the travelers in the van and they take advantage of it. The three men have been overpowered by the soldiers and are taken to the side of the road just off the checkpoint.

Still in view of everyone the guards execute the trio, cutting their throats with their own knives. A cascade of blood slips down the front of the first man and he falls to the ground. The other two watch and one of them starts to plead for his life. The man who killed the first soldier, reacts the oppositely and screams obscenities and cursing the guards. The cowering man is the next of the two to go, he doesn't fall over but instead leans on the last one. Gasping like a fish out of water, until finally he is at peace. As the guards get closer to the survivor and one of them places the cold steel to his flesh, the man summons all his strength and yells in his final breath, loudly so that all can hear. "RESISTANCE!" After that it all falls silent.

The man in the front seat breaks the silence in the van. "Death to Hope.." he mourns. "No…" Robert answers back. ".. The price of resistance."

At the last checkpoint, everything goes just as smoothly as the first. They get greeted by the guards and asked where they are going and why. He asks about the book like the other guards and Robert hands him the documentation. When he does this the plastic cover of his false tattoo over his real RFID mark gets hit by sun, reflecting it in the guards face. "Sir, we have a problem. I need you to exit the vehicle."

"Charlie when I say run, you get across the border. No matter what, you get to the border," Robert tells him. Charlie nods. Robert puts the book in Charlie's bag and hands it to him. More guards approach the men to assist with the search. One of them heads toward Charlie and this infuriates Robert. None of the guards see Robert reach behind him and the weapon he pulls out. This proves very unfortunate for the guard by Charlie especially. "Don't you dare touch my nephew. You puppet," he says to the guard. When the guard turns to face Robert he finds a pistol in his face. "HEY! You can't have one of th-." The gun goes off preventing the guard from finishing his statement.

"RUN! Charlie, get out of here! Get across the border, they will protect you there!" Charlie sees the border and makes a dash for it, miraculously avoiding getting hit by the taser projectiles and bullets being exchanged in the cloud of chaos.

A couple of feet from the border Charlie turns to look for Robert, just in time to see him hit in the chest with a continuous hail of projectiles. "NO!" Charlie screams, tears running down his face as the last person he knows falls to the ground. He sees his Uncles face as landing, he has the same glassy eyes as the bodies in the house. The electrical surges were too much for Robert's heart to take. Another of Charlie's relatives is dead.

"Charlie, what are you doing?" the driver shouts. "Get out of here!" Right after he falls down in seizures from a couple of tasers. Charlie turns back to his destination. A couple more feet are all that separate him from freedom. He feels a sudden sting in the back of his neck and reach back expecting to feel the barbs of a projectile, but instead his hand is covered with blood. One of the guards shot Robert's gun. From the forests lining the border comes the crack of gunfire and the guard that shot Charlie goes down dead. Other guards come to help but they are brought down before they can be of any assistance. "Charlie! Hold on, I'll get us across the border," says the man from the front seat.

"Charlie! Can you hear me? Char-" Charlie feels things start to become blurry and fade away, as he drifts into unconsciousness. It appears that failure is their destiny.

CHAPTER 4

"Charlie, wake up," comes an unfamiliar and gruff voice. "Good to see you back with us, son. We were worried that we were going to lose you too."

"What happened?" he asks, in a very small voice.

"One the guards shot you, but don't worry we got all of them. The other survivor brought you across the border. Welcome to Canada. We fixed you up here. You're unbelievably lucky, you shouldn't be alive from that shot. I think the only reason you survived was it hit your RFID."

"So my chip was destroyed?"

"Yes, I hope you weren't fond of it. The fact is it might have kept you from crossing the border anyway. The new models have a type of failsafe to keep the recipient in the country. It sends an electrical impulse in the spinal cord to incapacitate, but it is also a homing signal for the nanites in the body," he answers.

"Nanites?" Charlie asks.

"Nanites are micro robotic technology. Originally used for surgeries and other medical applications, but then the government started using them. Whenever you go to the hospital, even for simple inoculations more are introduced into the body. The plague of 2017 was a ruse to get everyone inoculated, the nanites were even implanted in with the vaccine."

"Wait a minute. We made it to Canada? We got across the Northern border, out of America? How do I get asylum?"

"Relax, relax. We already have it in the works. Your only job right now is to heal," the man said.

"What if I need you again?"

"Just use the intercom and call for me.. I'm sorry, I didn't introduce myself, did I? I'm Doctor Samuel Riddick," Dr. Riddick, says while holding out his hand.

"Charles Thayer," he says while weakly shaking the doctor's hand.

"Pleased to meet you, Mr. Thayer."

****

The doctor then leaves, letting Charlie get to rest. In the hall, he runs into the man from the van.

"Ohh! Travis you scared me," Riddick says.

"That was not my intention.. I came by to see him. How's he doing?"

"Very well actually. Most of his problems now will be psychological and emotional, not physical."

"What is our next move then?" Travis asks.

"For right now, nothing. The boy is not the only one who could use rest. Go back to your room. I'll call you when I need you."

"Doctor, you know who his uncle was right? The sacrifices he and his family made. I will not let them have died for nothing," he presses Riddick.

"I understand all that. I do. But it is not in anyone's best interest to act hastily. We need a calculated strategy, which we will discuss in a couple of days. Do YOU understand?"

"Yes, sir.." Travis replies, in a hushed voice.

"We will take it all back. We will get justice for the innocent who have given their lives for the cause. But be patient," Dr. Riddick says.

Travis just nods and reluctantly goes back to his room.

For the next few days Charlie just sleeps. It's still night when he does wake up. He gets up to get a drink of water. On legs that are still a little shaky, he wobbles to the door. Using the wall to steady himself, he walks down the dark hallway to a sink and finds a cup in a cabinet. He fills it and takes in the cold water. He starts to cough a little. Than a little more. Until a minor cough turns into an asthmatic episode. Desperately, he calls out for help. Barely able to talk, he falls to the floor grabbing at the pots and pans on the counter. Anything that he thinks will clatter as it accompanies him down. There is a loud ruckus from all the cookware and the dishes that he didn't see shatter. From the shadows his uncle Robert appears to save him again. Overjoyed to see his uncle again he doesn't notice the man behind, not until it's too late. He sees Robert lean forward in pain and fall down, a knife sticking from his back. It's a soldier that steps out from the shadow. "He can't save you this time," the soldier says. "We have poisoned you. Go ahead, call for help, there's no cure. There's nothing you can do. There's nothing anyone can do. You're dead all, each and everyone of you. You're all dead. You're all dead." Charlie gathers all his strength and tries to shout, but all that comes out is a pink foam. He starts spitting the foam out and tries again. Also in vain. He waits a couple of minutes, closes his eyes and tries one more time with success. The sound of his own cries scares even him.

When he opens his eyes, he sees he's still in the bed and hears footsteps from the hall coming to his room. Still in a state of panic he leaps from the bed and hides under it. It still hasn't sunken in that it was all a dream.

"Charlie? Charlie? Where are you, are you alright?" It's Dr. Riddick. Charlie recognizes the voice and crawls out from under the bed.

"Dr. Riddick, I thought I was going to be

killed. I was being poisoned by the water from the sink. A soldier came out and told me I was dead and there was no cure," Charlie frantically tells the Dr.

"Shhh… It's okay Charlie it was just a nightmare, that's all. American Armed forces can't touch you now, you're a refugee with asylum. If they tried, it would start a war. Besides, they don't know that you survived. They are not looking for you."

"What about the Clergy? Are they going to get me?" Charlie asks.

"The Clergy? How do you know about them?"

"His uncle Robert told him," Travis tells the Dr. "Charlie, my name is Marshall Travis. I didn't tell you my name sooner because, well, Robert's death was not part of the plan.

I used to be with the military, but I defected when I found out about what they and the Clergy were doing. What I was doing… Your uncle helped a lot of people to see what was going on. Now we are making it our mission to help the resistance."

"How are you feeling, Charlie?" Riddick asks.

"I don't know. Fine, I guess. Still scared," Charlie answered.

"I imagine that you will be scared for awhile. You have gone through a lot. More than anyone should. As well as being a doctor, I'm also an historian and I help educate those refugees who want to learn the real history of America. I'm a refugee too. I left the country before the time of the Overlords, about fifty years ago. I was twenty two. Even then we were in a totalitarian system."

"Totalitarian?" Charlie asks.

"Sorry.. A system where the government has full control of the lives of its citizens. You see, when the country was first set up its citizens got to decide what was right for them. Not the government. As time went by, the government intervened more and more."

"How did that work? I mean without the Overlord?" Charlie asks.

"We had what was called a President. Both he and the Senators were voted in by the citizens."

"No way. I don't believe you," Charlie says.

"It's true, Charlie. Didn't you ever think that maybe the Overlord and his minions might not have been straight forward with what's going on? Maybe what they said didn't add up?"

"No, the Overlord wouldn't do that. He looks out for us. He protects us from others and ourselves," Charlie states, sounding like a zombie.

"Have you been reading the book that you brought with you?"

"A little bit, yes," Charlie replies.

"What did you think?"

"It's a little hard to understand."

"It will be. It's never easy to alter your way of thinking. It can be very therapeutic though, if not at times necessary," Riddick says.

"Continue reading it. We also have other great books here for you as well. Feel free to read them. Let's go Travis." Travis, a little perplexed, follows the doctor out of the room.

"What are you doing, Sam? We need him to start his training."

"I just did. Look Marshall, let him make the first steps on his own. You're thinking like a soldier, treating him in that manner will scare him off. Right now he needs the soft hand. His whole world was completely destroyed, after all. He is involved in this without his consent, mind you. Trust me, this is best."

"Okay. This is your show," Travis replies, and he heads to the kitchen.

Charlie gets up out of bed and grabs the book. He opens it up and again starts reading.

"Law 3 for the Tyrant;
Another tool of oppression and the most effective. Control of all knowledge. If an individual finds a way to eliminate all competing ideologies and philosophies, and institute their own.

A truly vain dictator will claim that those in opposition to him are not a threat. Consider this, however, if that were true why mention such enemies, for such actions will not help him and in turn will embolden them.

More dangerous still is the tyrant who interferes in the responsibility of educating the young. He can make him an immortal or a martyr. He can poison the minds of generations that will take years to repair, if possible to do so."

The Nazis excelled at this. Hitler ordered the burning of books, art, poetry, anything contradictory to the Aryan doctrine was reduced to ashes. There was also the Hitler Youth, a squad of teenage killers and bullies, brainwashed into believing the Nazis and the Fuehrer could save them all. That he was their god. That he could do no wrong. It's scary what a warped ideology can do to people.

While many of the conquerors of other nations, Alexander the Great, Napoleon Bonaparte, were men considered of great civility and class. Breaking the bodies of other men, they left their hearts intact. They left the culture and art for others to study, enjoy, and learn from. But this is not for the Nazis. They made sure to kill the evidence of the others very exi-

stence. To them there could be no other civilization except theirs. Like the Huns and the Barbarians, that was their philosophy. Destroy and conquer.

Destroy and conquer. Destroy and conquer. Those words rang through Charlie's head over and over again. Charlie puts down the book and lays on the bed staring at the ceiling, thinking about what he has read. He feels his eyes get heavy and he drifts off to sleep.

When he wakes, the clock reads nine-thirty; he rubs his eyes and gets out of bed. He walks to the kitchen and fixes himself a bowl of cereal. With bowl in hand he walks to the window. This is the first time he had actually seen what surrounds the house, since he got there a week ago. Outside is a sight that he had never even known existed. A field of grass and trees are everywhere. There are mountains and a blue lake. A group of small birds, disturbed by some perceived predator, burst from the trees. He puts his free hand up to the glass watching it in awe.

"Amazing isn't it?" Dr. Riddick says while coming up behind the child. "Yes, it is," Charlie answers.

"How are you today, my boy?"

"Feeling pretty good."

"You look more alive.. Let's go outside.

You must being feeling stir crazy."

"Okay," Charlie replies.

Dr. Riddick opens the door and gently guides Charlie outside.

They are greeted by a light summer breeze and the crisp smell of vegetation. The chirps of the birds and splashing calls from the body of water that is only a few feet away. Sun is just starting to warm the air and only does more so as they step out of the shadow. Charlie starts walking toward the woods and feels the nearest tree, caressing the rough bark. "You've never been around trees like this have you?"

"No, I've heard about them. Supposedly the Industrial and Manufacturing Sectors of America are full of them... That's what we were told at least. Why did they lie to us?"

"They wanted to keep the country divided. If those of authority can convince the residents of the Capitol City that those in the outskirts are lying when they tell you the truth about the hor- rible conditions they live in, those well-meaning in the elitist society there, won't join their cause."

"Divide and Conquer?" Charlie asks.

"Yes," Riddick says.

Charlie watches a mantis snatch up a gras- shopper that gets too close.

"Charlie, there's something you should know... It's about your parents and uncle.. They are.." Riddick starts.

"They're dead aren't they," Charlie replies, as more of statement than a question.

"Your uncle is, but your parents aren't. Not yet, anyway. Their executions are scheduled for the end of the week," Riddick informs him. "I'm sorry."

A ladybug lands on Charlie's hand, almost like it too is trying to comfort him. He watches the insect walk up and down his arm until it flies away.

"Can anything be done for them?" Charlie asks.

"It's too dangerous, Charlie. Anyone who goes in would surely receive the same fate."

"Now, the boy has to hear this? Riddick has been trying to talk me out of going in after them for the past two days," Travis says, walking up to them, and addressing Charlie.

"I take it you're still considering that act of madness?" Riddick asks.

"You'd be right."

"I'll listen for your team's execution notices on the news."

Travis' only reply is to walk away.

"What a stubborn man. He's going on a suicide mission."

"You don't think he's right?"

"If he was going to save a group of people, that's a commendable act. Only a couple is an unreasonable risk. Even if they are some of the finest human beings I have ever known."

"You knew my parents?" Charlie asks.

"Briefly, but yes. I travel through America frequently and have some powerful connections. Your uncle we all knew, he helped a lot of people here to safety. Come on Charlie, let's go check out the lake." Riddick starts toward the lake and for a moment Charlie just sits there, thinking about what he heard. But his attention span, short, like all children, he doesn't dwell on this for long and runs to catch up with the doctor.

After exploring the lake, Charlie goes on to search for Travis. He finds him packing up his supplies. "Hi," Charlie says.

"Hey kid. What's up?"

"When are you leaving?"

Travis looks at his watch. "In a couple of hours."

"I don't want you to go."

Travis sighs. "Riddick is wrong. It's part of our responsibility to save the innocent. If it puts our lives on the line that's immaterial. As an officer, that is my duty."

"What were the duties of the officers that took them? Aren't they your officer brothers?"

"Not anymore," Travis replies glibly.

"Did you know that today is my birthday?"

"No, I didn't.." Travis responds, a little taken back by the change in topic. "How old are you?"

"Thirteen."

"Thirteen, and already seen so much death, felt so much pain. Happy Birthday."

"You know what I want for my birthday?"

"No. What?"

"Not to lose another person. My parents and Robert made a choice. They chose to sacrifice themselves for me. Riddick isn't wrong and it's not right for you to give your life for them so needlessly."

"Needlessly? That's your own family you're talking about."

"I've cried for them long enough. I will always miss them, but it's time to move on.. Please, don't go."

Travis sits down begrudgingly and looks down at the floor. After a couple seconds of silence, Charlie asks Travis a question. "When did you see your first dead body?"

"In my early twenties. It was in my first year as an officer, I was a senator's son too. But I was a lot more hot-headed than you. Eager, I wanted to serve my Overlord."

"What's wrong with that? Charlie asks, confused by the remorse in Travis voice.

"Everything. You should never sacrifice your life for a leader. Your country, your family, your freedom, yes, but never for your leader. When you live in that kind of society, it's a sign of how corrupt it has gotten."

"How many people have you killed?"

"Too many. At least now I'm fighting on the right side."

"As an officer you weren't? That doesn't

make any sense."

"As an officer I was supposed to protect the innocent and help improve their lives. I didn't do that. I was a puppet for the Overlord."

"Oh." Charlie replies, and sits there letting the silence return but only for a minute. "Do you have any more ice cream?"

"I don't know let's go check."

After Charlie helps Travis unpack they head to the kitchen and search the freezer.
"Rocky Road or Mint Chocolate Chip?" Travis asks.

"Mint," Charlie asks eagerly.

"Mint, it is."

Travis gets some bowls and dishes up the dessert. He puts the bowl and spoon in front of the child. "Did you know that ice cream is only allowed in the Capitol City in America?"

"Really? The people on the Industrial Sectors don't get ice cream? That's just wrong."

Travis smiles at this comment. "That's one of many injustices we hope to change," says Riddick, as he enters the house.

"Hi Charlie. Marshall, you decided to stay?"

"Yeah, the kid talked me into it."

"Good job, Charlie."

Riddick fixes himself a cup of tea, he pulls up a chair and sits by Charlie. "Have you ever killed anyone Dr. Riddick?"

"No, I have lost patients though. But kill

someone, no. Thank God," Riddick replies.

"What's that?" Charlie asks.

"What's what?"

"God? You said 'thank God'. What's God?"

This question obviously has Riddick concerned, putting a loosely closed fist up to his mouth. He then stands up and walks away.

"Dr. Riddick? Dr. Riddick, what's wrong?" Charlie then turns to Travis and asks him. "What did I do?"

"Nothing. Your question just freaked him out, that's all. He's not mad, not at you anyways. Give him a minute," Travis says, reassuring Charlie.

Charlie doesn't see Dr. Riddick for the rest of the day and spends it instead with Travis. They talk about their pasts and Travis tells him about what the city where they are residing is like. It was once a town of trade and later a metropolis because of the railroad industry of Canada, it was rebuilt. But in the winter of 2020 it was abandoned because of a major blizzard. When the first refugee Americans fled the country, it was one of the cities brought back to life. It was renamed Phoenix by its new colonists.

"How do you know all this? It was before you were born, some of it before Dr. Riddick."

Travis goes to one of the bookcases and grabs a book, *The History of Canada and the Americas: How Canada Become a Major Super-*

power Because of the United State's Collapse.

"What are the 'United States?'" Charlie asks.

"It's what America once was. A collection of individual governing entities, with their own cultures, their own laws, and their own representatives. United as a country, but strong because of their autonomy. Back then, Utah, Texas, Alaska and New Hampshire, were all parts of a much larger puzzle, instead of separate countries."

"Really? That's so cool."

"Yeah, I suppose it is," Travis replies.

"It's late, Charlie. You should go to bed."

"Okay. Good night, Travis." Charlie takes the book into his room. After Charlie closes the door to his room, Travis storms off to confront Riddick.

"What is wrong with you? That boy needs you and you go hide? Tell me what is going on in that head, because at times I'm completely baffled."

Riddick lifts up his arm and in his hand is a shot glass. Travis sees a liquor bottle on the table that is about half empty. "Want a shot?" he asks Travis, who doesn't say anything just continues to look at him still confused. "Too bad, it's the good stuff. Shame it's outlawed back home. I read a couple of chapters of that Legacy book. It tells about how a tyrant comes to power.

"Law 4 for the Tyrant:

*Of the greatest power is the final mani-
pulation. To become a God in human form.
That is the greatest Legacy. That's immortality
itself. Turning men away from all theologies
and placing their faith in their leaders of flesh.
This is the greatest of power and the hardest of
all evil to exorcise. This is the death of faith
and faith of any philosophy, in where the hearts
of men lie. The tyrant cannot allow faith to
flourish unimpeded."*

"I'm sorry about today, Marshall, but his
inquiry scared me. Scared me down to the bone.
I didn't know things there were that bad. You,
Robert, every refugee I've known knew of the-
ology in one form or another. I don't try to re-
cruit others to my faith, but a child knowing nothing of faith at all. That is one of the most des-
picable acts I've heard of. It got to me," Riddick
answers back.

Travis just nods and starts to walk off.
"Marshall, get some sleep. Tomorrow you start
training the students in hand to hand combat.
Vacation's over and we all go back to school."

CHAPTER 5

The next day Charlie is awakened by Dr. Riddick. "Dr. Riddick, what are you doing?" Charlie asks.

"It's time for school," Riddick says.

"UUHHHHH!!" Charlie groans, and pulls the sheets over his head.

"Come on, Charlie."

"Fine," Charlie replies.

"Well, that was easier than I thought it would be."

"The last person that I gave a hard time about waking me up will be dead soon. It was on the last day I saw her."

"Oh, I see.. Then let's go."

Riddick took Charlie downstairs into the basement. A bunch of other children are already there. "Go ahead and take an empty seat. Class, this is Charlie, he's now joining us."

Riddick goes to the front of the room and opens one of the books that are on his desk. He looks around the room and then down at the floor.

"A long time ago, I was an educator. I taught in a school in America for a couple of years, until I was told by the government that what I included in my curriculum was illegal. I refused to conform to their standards of knowledge. I took a stand, understanding full well what the repercussions of my actions could be. But I did it anyway and I would do it again if I could go back. If you learn nothing else from me, that's the most important one. Take a stand.

Do any of you know what this basement was originally built for? It was a bomb shelter from the second world war. Why did we need a bomb shelter? Yes, Shara?" Riddick says, gesturing to a girl with bright green eyes, about Charlie's age, sitting in the middle row.

"Because we believed that the Nazi's would bomb America after we entered the war."

"That's right. We didn't know if Hitler had the atomic bomb, since Albert Einstein was a German citizen before evading occupied Germany. We felt we had to take proactive steps to avoid destruction. Why did Einstein flee Germany?"

"He was Jewish and was going be killed by the Nazi's."

"Correct. I should note though, many are under the impression that Hitler created this hatred, but he didn't create it. He manipulated it. He utilized the distrust that was already in the mindset of Germany and other European nations, to validate the extermination of millions of people. This is what tyrants do. Take over your mind, body and soul. Turn all that is good on it's head and resell it to you in a new package. That's why we are here. To learn the lessons of history and right the wrongs that those before us allowed to happen."

Charlie raises his hand. "Yes, Charlie?" Riddick asks, giving him the gesture to proceed. "What you were saying about control of knowledge. Is that like when the Germans destroyed everything in countries they took over?"

"Yes, Charlie. That's it exactly. That is an old tactic, much older than the Third Reich. It isn't always towards a foreign society. One society that had a domestic version of this tactic, was ancient Egypt, where such tactics were even common. If the people or the new Pharaoh who came after the old Pharaoh who was already in power, were displeased with him, they would destroy all he had built. Every passage about him. Every mark on the temples. His own temple would be destroyed. He had to be erased from existence. His Legacy, was basically transformed into just a memory."

After their history and ethics lessons by Dr. Riddick the class moves outside for combat training with Travis.

It was a full day and everyone is tired. But it's a good tired, one with a feeling of accomplishment attached. Charlie, ever curious, doesn't let his fatigue divert him from his independent studies. As well as Legacy, he's reading the book recommended by Travis about America's history.

An avid reader he has been devouring the books and is already about fifty pages into the history book.

"How is it?" Riddick asks, when he comes to look in on the boy.

"Good… But I'm confused. Slavery, religious conflicts, the way the Jews were treated, I don't understand all this anger. It seems like a waste of time and energy. All the good they could have done if they had let all that go. Why were they all so unwilling to forgive and forget?"

"Well, that's hard to really explain, Charlie. Especially for someone who has the same attitudes about it as you do. I would guess that mostly it wasn't because of the people themselves, but their leaders that kept those fires of hatred burning. They had a specific agenda and in order to accomplish it they needed their supporters to stay fired up and ready to do whatever they ordered. They used propaganda. Propaganda is a very powerful thing, not to be underestimated. It will convince the masses to go against their very logic, give up all their freedoms and go against their own best interests. It's the tool of enslavement."

"Okay. I think I'll just keep reading to find out."

Riddick chuckles at this and tussles Charlie's hair. "Alright, my boy. Enjoy the books."

Charlie looks over at the other book on the bed. LEGACY. The cover looking more and more worn, but oddly enough the title seems to shine more brightly everyday.

He closes the history book and grabs Legacy instead and opens it to where he left off. For the most part he's been reading the 'Laws for Tyrants' headings more than the rest of the chapters.

"Law 5 for the Tyrant:

In order for a civilized society to prosper, it needs to adopt a policy of an equal mixture of Justice and Humanity.

To elaborate on this, I refer to Justice by the authority. When a crime is committed, under the Laws of Justice, all actions against the guilty are validated. No matter how heinous or painful the method of redemption (the form of punishment), is immaterial, as that is not a Law of Justice as long as balance is restored Justice is achieved. The Laws of Humanity, however, is one to temper this and the guilty are to be given mercy. In severe crimes, warranting the loss of the guilty man's life. With a quick death without malice and brutality. This way, all involved will get justice. The guilty will no longer be a threat to civil society and the loved ones on both sides will be at peace and can heal. This is the Law of Humanity satisfied."

Charlie puts the book down and walks to the window. As he look out at the into the night, he's bombarded by memories of lessons from his science classes.

The sun is a billion times larger than the earth. In turn the star, Arcturus, is a billion times the size of the sun. But the larger still is the star, Antares, which is a billion times the size of the star, Acturus. The instructor mentioned a couple of other stars but Charlie had forgotten their names. Even more, there are unknown numbers of stars out there that we don't know about that could be larger still. In the instructor's warped version of this lesson, he makes his students known that they are insignificant and that any thoughts of rebellion should be halted. It would ultimately end in defeat and their demise. A thought that has relevance for Charlie's current path.

The next morning before classes, Charlie asks Riddick his opinion on all this. "You want to know my opinion about the subject or your teachers' interpretation?" Riddick replies.

"Uhh.. Both," Charlie says, a little confused. He hadn't even given any thought to his former teacher's comments as being open for discussion.

"It's an excellent thought. Very provocative. It's important to stay humble, think that you might be wrong. It keeps you honest and open to the opinions of others. His conjecture on the topic is kind of paradoxical to his original point though. He's making a statement that our egos should not get in the way of our journey of knowledge, but then he made a followup that is a barricade to open debate, by posing a perceived threat to your life.

Whether legitimate or not doesn't matter, if your opinion matters to you and you can defend it, then do that. Let others decide it's legitimacy in practical application. Don't let fear of possible consequences stifle you into submission."

"So you're saying the only way to really lose is if you let others silence you?" Charlie asks.

"Well said, Charlie. That's it exactly."

"What is today?" Charlie asks.

"Thursday, why?"

"Tomorrow is my parents execution isn't it?"

"Yes. It is, Charlie. I'm sorry."

Charlie doesn't say anything and just follows Riddick to the classroom. In class he silently listens to the subjects without contributing.

While he doesn't have problems with the combat training, it's not his favorite class and he usually enjoys the intellectual exercises far more. Today, though, he's actually really looking forward to the tactical maneuvers, fresh air, and physical exertion. The odd thing is in his distracted emotional state his focus seems enhanced, not hindered. His endurance on the other hand suffers greatly and he needs a break about half-way through the class.

At the end of the day, Charlie is very tired and doesn't open either of the books, but instead listens to the music from the radio. It's been a week without the announcements and although he has always hated them, in another way he misses them. Not the announcements themselves, but it being part of a routine. A part of his old life. A life that has been becoming a memory until today. The gentle sounds of the jazz music that he listened to at home, is bringing on the nostalgia. He feels a very welcomed sleep equal only to that he got when he first got here.

From his unconscious state he receives vision-like dreams, like ghosts he sees his parents faces and even Robert. They're all not back there though. Not in America, but here, at Charlie's new home. A place where he feels safety for himself and his family. No Overlord. No soldiers. No death and pain. Not the pageantry of destruction that he had known from before, just his family and him.

The running through the fields of grass. There, a gathering of monarch butterflies were feeding on the pollen in the flowers woven in the natural tapestry, part in flight. Almost on cue they all take off at once making this orange and black cloud.

He climbs the trees while his family of apparitions watches him, he puts his ear to its trunk.

The jazz music is coming from the tree!

Without having to change clothes they are all in their swimwear and run into the lake swimming in the deeper parts and splashing around. Hitting a ball that appears back and forth among them. Now the music is coming from the water, replacing the natural orchestra of the lake. It's an amazing dream, the sights and sounds. A needed distraction from reality.

They are now at the patch of bare ground near the lake. His mom is starting a fire and the men are fishing from the lake, just like they used to do. They cast out the line, not immediately catching anything. Charlie casts out again and feels a tug on the line. He pulls and pulls, preoccupied he hasn't noticed the music stopping. Almost have it. One more big pull and it comes flying at them. Charlie grabs his catch and holds it up. Pulling the hook out he sees something in the fish's mouth.. some foreign object. He reaches in and using the side of the animal's jaw he maneuvers the object, bringing it up the throat. He gets to feel it for the first time. It's soft, smooth, and a little damp. It reminds him of the feel of a shelled egg.

Dark clouds come rolling in and the wind picks up. His family urges him to go with them to the car, but he's determined to find out what this fish has swallowed. It starts to rain, but he doesn't leave his spot. With one more large tug he gets it loose, he's got it in his closed fist. He opens his fist and finds himself staring down at a human eye. He drops the fish and the eye, and while backing away he falls down himself. A few short feet from the fish he sees it's not jumping around in fits, like the other fish he's gotten before. It's just laying there. At first he thinks it's dead. Then it starts to open it's mouth, then it closes it again. It repeats this for a couple more times, until Charlie notices a sound coming from the fish. Faint at first, as it continues, it gets louder and louder. It's laughing! Not a joyous laughter either, but a very maniacal, disturbing sound. It reminds him of the squealing call of the hyenas at the zoo his uncle took him to last summer. It suddenly stops laughing and opens it mouth again and speaks. It says but two words, in an equally disturbing tone. "What's God," it mocks. The fish then makes one giant leap and lands in the water. For the first time he notices the change of the weather and sees the rain, but it's not rain water, it's raining maggots. With this sight, he runs to join the others at the car.

They hear a twig snap and the shadows appear. He can't see who they are or hear their voices but he doesn't have to. He knows all too well, who they are. He also knows it doesn't matter if they had actually committed a crime. Since they are here, they are all in danger. They start the car and drive off, heading as fast as they can away from the shadows. Faster and faster they go, traveling back across the border.

They drive into the industrial section of the country, where Charlie sees the little girl he saw during his trek out of America. As they get closer, she gets more and more skinny, until she turns into a skeleton. Still standing, she lifts her bone arm and points the way they are going.

On the road they are traveling is a never ending industrial section, seeing horror after horror. Fighting between soldiers and civilians. Suddenly a bridge appears. They enter the darkness of it, and are greeted by a dark they have never known, like being in space. When back in the light, a new scene is playing out around them. It's still a war, but from a jungle.

Machine gun fire surrounds them from soldiers whose faces they can't see. They can make out their uniforms, though, which includes a wide pointed hat that looks like a wok cooking pan. They are in the jungles of Vietnam. The foursome in the car are not dressed in their modern clothing, but as South Vietnam civilians and the shadow figures in pursuit are in the uniforms and weaved hats. A fire blast erupts in front of them and people are running around on fire.

As they pass, Charlie sees the charred remains of a soldier, move his arm up pointing the way road are traveling, just like the little girl.

Up ahead is another tunnel and upon leaving it, a new battle field emerges. This time it's in occupied Germany. Again their clothing has changed to tattered rags with the star of David sewn on them. The shadows that were chasing them now were in Nazi uniforms, but still without faces. They drive through Auschwitz, and Soviet Russia until they reach another tunnel, and ended up in Germany during the first world war.

Now dressed as U.S. Military and the Shadows with the pointed hats of the Kaiser. They find another tunnel and at the end of it, the American revolutionary war is raging. This time they are wearing their modern dress and better still, the shadows are not behind them.

But they keep going, until suddenly their car is hit by cannon fire. Charlie is flung from the vehicle, when he looks over he sees it's on fire. Three burning bodies are lying on the ground by it. It's his family. As they turn to ashes he sees movement coming from them and rats, one after another burst from the ashes.

Charlie turns around sensing a presence coming toward him and the swarm of rats flee-ing from the wreckage. It's the shadow figures, and they start chasing the rats. The last one hit is by a cannon, possibly the one that's projectile hit their car. "They're only Vermin," he says to him, pointing ahead. It steps with the others and they all start stepping on the rodents. After it kills a couple of the rats, it menacingly approach-es him. That's when Charlie wakes up in a sweat and shaking. He pulls the covers over himself, but doesn't sleep for the rest of the night.

The next day Charlie is the first one up, giving up on sleep after his nightmare. He sits in the kitchen looking out the large windows at the rising sun.

"Charlie. Good morning. You're up pretty early, aren't you?" Dr. Riddick asks.

"I had another nightmare." He goes on to tell his dream to Riddick.

"That's quite a dream. What do you think it means?" Riddick asks

"I was hoping you could tell me," Charlie laments.

"Dreams are a very personal thing. I could tell you my impressions, but ultimately you have to figure it out. Don't stress out about it too much, son. As horrifying as they can be, most of the time is a dream is just that, a dream. An interpretation from our unconscious trying to tell us something our conscious might have missed. If you don't feel like going to class today, you don't have to."

"No. That's okay, I'll be there."

"That's good. The sooner you get back up, the better."

Once they got downstairs and joined the others, Charlie was already feeling better. He even made a couple of comments today. In combat training, he also did better. It appears his stamina has already improved.

As it got dark and the day comes to a

close, Charlie sits on the porch and is just enjoying being outside. He thinks about what Riddick said earlier. The sooner you get back up, the better. The request he's going to make is based on this and even thinking about it makes him cringe.

"Dr. Riddick, I have a favor to ask.." Charlie starts.

"Yes, what can I do for you?"

"This might sound weird but can we watch tonight's executions."

"Are you sure about that, Charlie?"

"You said that the sooner 'I get back up, the better.' You're right. I need to deal with this head on. Maybe then I can finally move on."

"You've suffered very traumatic events, at a young age. No one will blame you if you have a hard time dealing with them."

"I know. But I want to move on."

"If that's what you want. It will start in a couple of hours."

"We'll have dinner then and turn it on the American National News, I'm sure the Ultranet will be covering it."

In quiet anticipation of dread, the usually talkative Charlie, just sits and eats his portion of the turkey casserole Riddick fixed them. Being anxious for tonight, but not really in the slightest way eager, the minutes have suddenly started to drag to a slow crawl. For Charlie this is unadulterated torture.

Before searching for the executions on the

Ultranet, they look for other random videos. The "what's popular" sections, "recommended for you" sections, and "humor."

At about fifteen minutes to the event, Riddick punches in the ghastly topic in the search box. In no time at all they find. *Coverage of American Executions for Tonight.* "Last chance.." Riddick reminds Charlie. Charlie just nods and Riddick clicks on one of the highlighted subjects.

"Well, the celebrities just keeping coming out in droves for this one," says the announcer, smiling his masquerading and practiced smile.

"It appears the senator and his wife were very popular," says the female counterpart.

"Or they're glad to see them go," the male announcer, quips.

"Oh you're terrible!" she says, in mock anger.

For the next few minutes, that's the kind of comments Charlie has to deal with. Snide mockery, by social sycophants who are the judges of what is important. Ignoring what is real and tearing into anyone who has the imagination or analytical skills to have an independent thought. In this fake world that Charlie has left behind, he now sees how truly plastic such people can be.

The horns blow, calling the mockery and paltry banter between the manufactured monarchy, to a cessation. The lights are turned off with the exception of a spotlight that has been following a higher ranking officer who is walking up the stage. He steps onto the stage and up to the microphone in the middle of the stage.

"Ladies and Gentlemen, we come together in an collected act of uniform dedication to the Overlord. The actions of those in authority are particularly troubling since they know the gravity of their actions. In taking justice from the hands of the Overlords and creating their own version of law and order, creating dissent between the citizens and it's gracious Overlord, cannot be tolerated. To further enhance the gravity of this, these traitors will not be hanged.. But instead beheaded. The only reward for treason is death. Now onto the national anthem. LONG LIVE OVERLORD TYMES." Following the last statement comes the routine echo from the crowd. The camera scans the audience for the most enthusiastic for their close ups.

After the speaker has vacated the stage, a woman in her twenties steps out from the shadows and onto the stage and up to the microphone. In an angelic voice she performs a flawless performance of the national anthem. After the anthem the audience roars to life in an exuberant applause. The woman exits the stage and the spotlights land on a new location on stage, the stocks for 'political subversives' as the Overlord and his minions would call them. The stocks are black with a slightly visible coat of dried blood around the edges of the neck pieces.

Other than that, the pieces are very clean and ornate, obviously made for the aristocracy who stepped out of line. The bases have filigree and images of the noble lion and other such designs of the Overlords' realm.

The orchestra plays the Execution Ballad and the condemned are forced to march out on the stage. This time is different from the other executions Charlie had seen. This time the Overlord wants to make a real point.

His parents are naked and have obviously been tortured for the past week. Both have lost weight and are dirty. Not only dirt and grime cakes their bodies, but dried blood. Even through all that muck, the word TRAITOR, can still be visible on their skins. It was burned on.

Charlie starts to shake and Riddick starts to turn off the monitor. "NO.. DON'T!!" Charlie screams. "Charlie-" Riddick starts. "I have to watch it," Charlie interrupts. Riddick nods in acquiescence.

The crowd starts chanting, "DEATH TO THE TRAITORS," others hiss, and from the crowd comes a few projectiles. All the good the couple has done for the country has been forgotten. They will be remembered now as traitors, this is their Legacy.

The two officers that have been following the couple to the stocks, place them in their positions. They stand up, salute, and exit the stage. From the shadows of the stage come two large men holding equally large axes. From head to toe, they are dressed all in black and seem almost to have no real distinct forms.

This is what Charlie's dream was about. His parents' executions. His parents are not crying or carrying on like many of the other executed have. An expression of clear defiance is shining through their fatigue.

The executioners get in position and the camera follows the blades up and its journey down. To the surprise of everyone with their last strength the couple shout, "RESISTENCE."

The axes continue to the targets unobstructed, and the camera angle has changed to face the couple. Charlie watches in horror as he sees his parents disembodied heads bounce on the platform like a couple of beach balls. With her last nerve impulse Mrs. Thayer's eyes flutter and a single tear runs down her cheek.

Charlie turns and hides his face in Dr. Riddick. Riddick just strokes the boy's head of hair; they watch the frivolous after show, more with a sort of needed detachment than giving it real attention. The interviews are of the celebrities in attendance and showing those loyal to the empire's euphoric expressions, as they dine on the reserved decadent fares. No one in the crowd even take notice of the executioners moving the bodies and hosing the blood off the stage. Then the fireworks start and the cameras fix on that.

"Oh, how they reveal and delight.. In

such a glorious death of another human being. Decay and destruction is their home, and anyone who's not in unwavering allegiance is an enemy," Riddick says.

It falls on deaf ears, Charlie is just trying not to scream.

The next morning, Riddick finds Charlie to again be the first one in the kitchen. "Hi Charlie. Did you have another nightmare?"

"No, I wanted to watch the sunrise is all."

"Really?"

"It's a very beautiful sight," Charlie answers.

"Yes, it is. Yes, it is."

After the executions there has been a change in Charlie. He's become a better student and more focused. Riddick is concerned that in his state he might get distracted from the ethical implications of his actions, and start to sink into the trap of vengeance. To remedy this he refers him to literature that will remind him of his duty to humanity. Riddick must not fail at this, or Charlie could become the very monster they seek to kill.

CHAPTER 6

It's been ten years now since the executions of the Thayers and Charlie has become quite the warrior and scholar. The fears that Riddick had wound up being for not, because Charlie was determined to make his parents proud. The same attitudes about tempering justice with humanity would have been a philosophy that his parents cherished. But sadly their name had to be abandoned and at Riddick's urging Charlie did precisely that. After reading the origin of species he went with the new alias of Charles Ambrose Finch. He always liked the name of Ambrose, so that's why he included it in his new name.

He's also on a way toward a family himself. The girl with the bright shining eyes, Shara, has been an exhilarating partner for him.

She has only the one name that she is known as, even by Charlie. No one knew her parents and she refuses to tell her last name. Nobody really pressed her on it because everyone figured it must have been really traumatic, she was found at a crime scene at the age of five. She is Charlie's equal in weaponry skill and wit. Their relationship has already advanced from the child's innocence to the adult knowledge and they've been living together as common-law husband and wife for about four years now. They have one child together, a little girl two years old.

About that time, sadly, Charlie's mentor and the town leader Riddick died from cancer.

"Charlie? Why are you up so early?" Shara asks, as he fixes himself breakfast.

"Travis and I are going down to the Republic of Utah. There was an incident and the Utah congress has requested our presence."

"What happened?"

"That incident, in Las Vegas, a couple of months ago when a visiting Utah dignitary and his family were killed. The Utah congress declared war.

Last night, Texas was bombed. The Overlord was trying to keep Texas from becoming an ally with Republic of Utah. The investigation has shown evidence that the Clergy had something to do with the attacks. We will be gone a couple of days."

Charlie kisses her goodbye, then into his daughter's room looking at her sleep for a moment before kissing her on the head. He walks out the door finding that in perfect timing Travis is already waiting.

"Ready?" Travis asks.

"I guess so."

So they begin their journey in relative silence. On the way there, Charlie reads through the reports of the incident and asks Travis questions about it. After crossing into the American border they have to navigate through a series of border crossings. Nowadays more of a hassle, than the life and death scenario of ten years ago.

With their Canadian citizenship in place, they can't be arrested by the Clergy or the Transportation Department authorities, or whatever department heads they come across. They can, however, be harassed by them. Where Charlie's RFID chip once was, is now but a burn mark that had healed over a long time ago. A reminder for Charlie to never let his guard down. As the authorities search them and their belongings, a woman and her child are taken away by the guards. Their fate is unknown but most likely unpleasant.

Getting through the entry checkpoints, they start their journey to the country within a country. Charlie and Travis have not only made quite a name for themselves with the resistance, but also within the realm of politics. Travis is high-ranking in military circuits in Canada and Charlie has been groomed for a career as a Senator.

Now at the border of Utah, they have no more checkpoints to go through and go to the Utah Embassy. They are greeted by their attendant who leads them to the congress that is getting ready. They greet the different senators and other representatives of the country of Utah and the other countries, New Hampshire, Texas, and Alaska, all have been asked to attend. The head of the congress hits his gavel to get everyone's attention. "Order, order. Let's get on with the session. Senator Lundberg of Texas has the floor."

"Thank you, your honor. Fellow representatives. Last night, as you know there was an attack on the country of Texas. This only a short time after the assassination of a Utah senator, while visiting Las Vegas, America, Sector three. Our investigation, with the help of Texas' investigators, have found a connection between the attacks and the Overlord's Clergy Force. We call this session in response to this and implore the countries of Alaska and New Hampshire to join us and make a formal declaration of war.

At one time our countries were states and we all know the reasons we separated from that union. Returning to the laws that our founders had created after the Presidents ignored those amendments at times of inconvenience.

In the year 2014, the last president granted our request for secession to avoid civil war and for years that has been achieved. Now the tenuous truce has been violated and I say we need to respond. The War has already come, we might as well make a formal acknowledgement of that."

"The chair recognizes senator Kyle of Utah."

"Thank you, your honor. Senator Lundberg, thank you for your comments.

In the inquiry it was discovered that the

Labor Unions, with their Gestapo style tactics of law and order, let the Utah assassination occur. Las Vegas has always been prosperous, despite their influence. But they have gone too far. This was not an isolated incident and evidence shows that they are in league with the Overlord.

I'm not a reactionary man. I have always asked for a cool head in these matters. But we are in the middle of a war. Let's show them that."

"The chair recognizes senator Bruinhill of Alaska."

"Thank you, your honor. Fellow senators. I'm not insensitive to what has transpired in the past few months, but for us in Alaska this is frankly not our concern.

We have always lived as an isolated refuge, even from the rest of America, when we were part of the United States. I believe this to be the best course for us. I urge my fellow Alaskan representatives to vote no on the declaration of war."

"The chair recognizes senator Lundberg for rebuttal."

"Thank you, your honor. So, you see the looming threat of war, and you don't feel the need to protect yourselves? War is on ALL our door-steps. Overlord Tymes will not see that distinction of philosophies between us and will feel the need to eradicate us all. Your reaction to all this is, let it happen?

I understand your desire to stay out of this, but at this current juncture that stance is one of self demise."

"Senator Kyle any rebuttal?"

The senator just waves no in response.

"Alaska's not going to join," Charlie says quietly, to Travis.

"What makes you think that?"

"I've read up on Senator Kyle. He holds a large influence in their legislature and the others won't go against him."

"That's too bad. We could really use their help."

"He's not wrong though either. I would have done the same thing."

"No you wouldn't," Travis says, obviously annoyed by that last remark.

"Alaska doesn't have a real stake in this. Not yet anyway. There is nothing for them to gain and everything to risk here. In the end, this debate right now is irrelevant. Alaska will be attacked and eventually have to pick a side.

It's New Hampshire, that's the wildcard here. Will their representatives step up now, or after?"

The debate continues on for another couple of hours, until a little after six. It is convened until tomorrow morning. The New Hampshire representatives have continued their silence through all this.

Charlie and Travis have a couple of drinks and dinner in the dining hall of the hotel. They offer to pay for their lodgings, but are informed that it has been taken care of. So they retire to their rooms for the evening.

The next day's session is the same as the day before. At the end of the sessions, all the participants return without any changes in their opinions. No one knows what New Hampshire is going to do.

As they travel home from the sessions, the American news brief interrupts the music.

"Rumors have flooded the country concerning the attacks that have been committed on the Republic of Utah and the country of Texas. The supposed Clergy, that have not been proven to even exist, were blamed for the attacks and have been said to have ties to Overlord Tymes. A spokesman for Overlord Tymes called such claims, "obvious and egregious lies, spread by the rebels to further their cause. They want to destroy everything, that's all.

In further news.."

"Different day, same story," Charlie replies.

"What?" Travis asks.

"It reminds me of one of the Laws of the Tyrant in Legacy.

Law 6 for the Tyrant:
Beware those in charge to inform the citizenry of the countries' affairs. Watch for praise and adulation of it's leaders, they might be in

collusion with the monarchy, or have lost their objectivity.

Either way they have made themselves a danger to the liberty of the people.

This is a place of tyranny."

****

Things played out as Charlie had predicted. Alaska voted "no" on a declaration of war, New Hampshire voted "yes". A month later the Clergy bombed the capitol city of Anchorage.

In response, the Alaskan congress makes a formal declaration of war.

Travis is called to help out the Alaskan army, but Charlie gets a reprieve and isn't needed on this trip. With this vacation, he spends the time with his family.

Travis goes out and teaches the troops hand to hand techniques, firearms, and survivalist training. Making sure they have all the advantages in the upcoming incursions against the American troops. While illegal for civilians and the police guards and soldiers, the military are still allowed firearms. They have also been ingrained with the doctrine of kamikaze, giving your life for your leader. This makes them that much more of a threat to their foes.

Travis instructs his pupils, in the training he received as a Green Beret. Training them what is eatable, how to get water and methods of camouflage. He instructs them in trapping, stripping down all kinds of firearms and how to disarm your opponent. His goal is to teach them how to survive in any set of circumstances, predictable or not, alone or as a unit.

He is encouraged by their eagerness and quick ability to learn. He tells Charlie about the strides they are making and that the troops should be ready in three months or so. Then he will go to assist in Utah, then New Hampshire, then Texas, and lastly the Canadian troops. If the other's trainings go this smoothly all the nation's involved should be ready to go before the year is out. The bad news is the Overlord's forces are always ready. In military society, war means power and control.

In an effort to diminish their resolve, the Overlord has set the Clergy out to attack America's neighboring nations. It has not diminished it at all, but to the contrary strengthened it. The brutal onslaught only encourages their united determination to bring down the tyrant, and the residents of the Industrial Sector are even enlisted as defectors and informants.

The resistance forces within the American borders have escalated their efforts and started performing espionage tactics. Bombings and fires are now being set by them in retaliation to the actions of the Clergy's attacks.

Government buildings and government Ultranet sites are hacked into, disabling them for days or weeks. Outbreaks of spontaneous violence erupt all over the country. When military drones are sent in to take out the threats, the drones are neutralized. Using either drones manufactured by the resistance with cell phone parts, or by artillery, the military drones are destroyed.

The propaganda of supposed spies that the Overlord's Information Department had been claiming for years is now true.

Reports of the dissidents have been spreading like a forest fire, emboldening the everyday man within America.

The Capitol City residents on the other hand are hit with a hurricane of half-truths and flat out lies by the Information and Propaganda Department. Reports have been saying that these are only isolated incidents by a few unruly anarchists and not an outpour of public sentiment against the Overlord. In their state of utter adoration to the Overlord, the citizens of the Capitol City eat this up. They have total faith in their leader and refuse to believe that he would lead them astray. All this contention is written off as lies by a bunch of malcontents; along with the 'myths' of the Caucasian Genocide, the era of the United States, or that the citizens once elected their leaders that were called 'Presidents.'

Charlie has been called to a meeting in Texas, to review the new Legacy policies established to watch for tyrants. He's always a little nervous when he has to go across the border and is afraid he will get recognized somehow. But for the past couple of years of doing this he has had nothing but success so far.

Aside from dealing with touchy and power-addicted Transportation Department Officers, his travel goes fairly smoothly. He makes a couple of stops in the Industrial Sector and visits with a group of workers. He drops off donations to them himself, as he researched the Charities and Welfare Department personally and found good reasons to be suspicious. He discovered that the money and donated goods were going into the pockets of the Overlord and those whom he paid off.

He helped out who he could without drawing too much attention to himself, intervention by visiting dignitaries was still discouraged and could have dire consequences for those he helped. He has diplomatic immunity and has nothing to fear, but those he encounters are not so lucky.

He sees the same gruesome sights he has seen in past travels and even with his diplomatic immunity, he dares not test his luck with the soldiers. They have a reputation of ignoring those laws, amongst other ordinances, so even he has to tread lightly. The announcement of war between the countries has only made things worse and the officers have gone from a mild hostility to a wave of contempt of foreigners.

The visitors from the other nations have been feeling more strained as well because of a change in policies of trade. The introduction of even higher tariffs and taxes have been placed on the other nations who respond by shutting down all trade. The already hurting people in the Industrial Sections now have to cope without the expensive goods from other countries. Not being able to afford the American high prices, theft has increased.

All this has made the emotional and psychological strains from those involved downright palpable. Do-gooders like Charlie have been trying to repair the damage between the Americans and foreigners as best they can. He knows how valuable to the cause they could be, and making sure they know they are not as alone as the Overlord and his forces want them to believe is the key.

As he reaches his destination, he sees where the country has suffered attack. Buildings are blackened and charred. Many are still the skeletal remains of the functional and flourishing city, waiting to be demolished and rebuilt.

Charlie makes his way to the Texas congress and enters the building. He meets with their dignitaries and meets the new senators. There are only half a dozen other senators from other countries at this meeting. Most have formed their own Legacy committees and these are their members.

"Order, Order. This session of the Texas congress is now convening. Thank you for your attendance." The meeting begins with the Texas pledge and singing of their anthem. Then the new senators are introduced and the business of the gathering is begun.

"Now, Senator Marcus from Texas has the floor," the speaker announces.

"Your honor, fellow senators, thank you for your attendance. Alaska, The Republic of Utah and New Hampshire, have had discussions about the Legacy policies and the implementation of the policies in their legislature.

It is still too early to see the results of this at this time, but the future impact from this change looks promising. The argument for the implementation, here in Texas is the agenda of this session.

Here to talk to us about the Legacy policies is Senator Charles Ambrose Finch, the creator of the Legacy papers."

Charlie swallows hard and stands up.

"Senator Marcus, fellow senators, thank you.

First of all, saying I'm the author is not entirely accurate. I'm just a humble senator from Canada. I discovered documents that I referenced to create protocol for freedom in countries that are in serious need of it. The major step in this is being able to recognize the inception of tyranny in the country and how best to counteract it. I don't claim that these are foolproof but with these guidelines, liberty for the citizens can be protected.

If you can recognize these traits in your representatives, than you can act before the damage can be done. Thank you."

Charlie sits down.

"The floor recognizes Senator Lundberg."

"Thank you, your honor. Senator Finch, I have read your Legacy documents and I contest that while they are sound policies, the argument in favor of it's implementation is.. weak.

I recommend another accompanying document, more strongly arguing for it's inception."

"Call for a vote on this?"

"Called," says one of the senators.

"Seconded?"

"Seconded," says another one of the senators.

"Let the vote proceed. Click your vote green for yes, red for no, on your electric ballot box."

The votes are cast and the outcome showing on the monitor on the wall. Ten in favor, five against. The motion passes.

"The floor recognizes Senator Lundberg again."

"Thank you, I wanted to add that I think the one who wrote the original document, should also author this document as well."

"All in favor."

This time there is only one vote against it and, it's the suddenly overwhelmed Charlie.

Chapter 7

Charlie takes the responsibility of this task to heart. This document is more than just to protect nations from tyrants, it's also a declaration of war against the American Empire and it's inhumane leader. A document making a sound argument for war for the records is a huge job for a senator with such limited amount of experience. This is only his second year as a senator. He searches book after book to find the right things to say. Included he rereads Legacy. He then finds a passage that will help.

Law 7 for the Tyrant:
You can convince the masses to give up everything and anything. All their hard-earned earthly possessions and goods. Their ethics even, with the proper introduction of a political sacrificial lamb. A totem of all in physical form, of all the cancerous parts of their civilization.

With this entity in place, the tyrant can get the citizens of his realm to abdandon their rights under his new rule.

In the Germany that my father knew under the Nazi reign, this principle could not be more evident. The Jew was nothing. The Jews were the inferior ones. This was an attitude of the people before Hitler, he simply utilized it into a weapon of hate.

Suddenly inspired Charlie starts writing:

In our own history, genocide has occurred. It is that of the Caucasian Genocide. It's flawed validation was the outbreak of a plague in 2017, that led to the mass hysteria with the outcome we all know. It was the concise and calculated extermination of the white man. The country of America has a strong history of racial division, with the white man shouldering the majority of the responsibility of it.

This is a long lived animosity and has utilized the rage from the descendents of slaves, for political purposes. This is an attitude, that to this day, still leaves many in confusion. Why feel guilt for the acts of your father's father? If you kill someone, should your children be held responsible for it. No, that would be absurd, but that is what the country was being asked to do.

This is only one of the crimes of Overlord

Tymes, but this most horrendous act is not alone outside his modus operandi. He has a recognized behavior pattern of this type of absolute control. Until now, it has for the most part, been a wound left to fester. That can no longer be the case, not because we say so, but because the Overlord and his cohort's actions dictate it.

The citizens of America have had to live on the table scraps, as this is his way to keep power.

Because of the actions of the first and second Overlords, we were all almost under this same rule, through the implementation of the Global Economy. This is not a new idea and has not worked and never will work. With evidence from what had happened before, the global economy was the worst conceived proposal they could have come up with. With the break-up of the European Union (now Central China and New India) in 2014 and the consequences of it as a shining example, the global economy was killed.

From start to finish, its conception was set to fail. The countries that would have benefited the most from the merge of nations refused to enter this pact. Their leaders had no trust in those who proposed the policy. The end result of America's endorsement of it and entrance into it wound up being the nation's downfall.

Once China, amongst others, refused to enter the 'Globalization Pact' and held America to its financial obligations it first hit the economy and then it struck militarily. This was the final step to the downfall of the country. It was brought about internally, with those whose duty it was to protect it involved.

Now Overlord Tymes wants to resurrect this agenda. Enslave us all to his eternal war machine, his eternal poverty. This is the only way he can keep control. These are his reasons for keeping the conflicts going. Our reasons for war are to counter him and neutralize the damage done by this despot. His regime has backed us to the wall and shown us we can no longer coexist in peace. The only option has become one of defense. If we had had the Legacy doctrine in place, the signs of the Tyrant would have been clear. We could have prevented this from happening in America. We are at the point when we must intervene.

They are the Laws for the Tyrant, twelve principles that must be observed to dissolve the power of the tyrant. The Laws are as follows…

He ends the document with the twelve 'Laws for the Tyrant' verbatim, from the LEGACY book.

When done, Charlie sets down the notepad and pen and rubs his tired eyes. From the Texas hotel, he looks out the large windows across the landscape. As well as this country he can see the ravages of America. From the fires burning across the country, he sees billowing pillars of smoke. When he opens the window the faint whiff of smoke drifts in and the falling ash can be seen. The sounds of the marching soldiers across the border in America, is faint but still there. The specter is an assault on all the senses. Charlie is suddenly really missing his home, so far away from all of these sensorial obscenities.

The next day Charlie presents his arguments to the Texas congress. The other senators listen intently showing random nods of acknowledgement and from others expressions of disgust. When he finishes there is a brief moment of silence, but this lasts only a couple of seconds and then the other senators are eager to put their perspectives into the political mixing bowl.

As expected there is an extreme mix of comments; from poignant and relevant, to extremist or absurd, to the down-right self-serving. The banter continues on for a couple of hours, until finally the document is approved and sent out to foreign lands. A few copies go overseas to the United Kingdom, Mexico and parts of New India and The Central Chinese Empire.

Sent later that night, by detractors, the rest are scattered across America. With the new trade restrictions causing the population to suffer from price increases, right now is the time to strike with this manifesto.

The night's business is through and the

senators adjourn to the dining hall to celebrate the evening with drinks and cigars. Along the wall is a table, set up with enough food to feed a small army. It's the kind of spread that Charlie was used to as the son of a senator. Shrimp, lobster, sweet bell peppers, mangoes, pineapples, grapes, and the usual food for those in the Capitol City, that are outlawed in rest of the country.

A sudden tinge of guilt hits Charlie at the sight of all this. Even though he knows it is not his fault he does feel a certain amount of responsibility for standing back and doing nothing while in the Capitol City. He steps outside and looks out across the landscape; so familiar, yet somehow alien, at the same time. He gulps down the contents of his glass and throws the glass in anger.

"Senator Finch, is anything wrong?" comes a voice from behind him.

"Senator Lundberg, no. I guess I needed to get some air is all.."

"It looks like you dropped your glass," Lundberg says, with a smile on his face.

"Something like that," Charlie says, and turns to look inside the filled room. "You know, as a child I grew up in the Capitol City. I attended functions like this all the time. I didn't even think about being a child of privilege and the suffering of those across the country."

"How could you? You didn't even know about it. The Capitol propaganda department made sure, that to you it was a myth.

As for your guilt for your childhood, you should take solace in the actions of your parents. From their perch of privilege they did more to help the common man than anyone. That's why your father became a senator and why he put everything at risk when he discovered what was going on. You have their strength you know. But you also seem to feel their guilt. You shouldn't. You're the product of a corrupt system, not the cause."

"Maybe," Charlie answers.

"Come on back inside. We have some people for you to meet." Lundberg puts his arm around Charlie and guides him back inside.

"Senator Finch, this is Michael Schultz. He's an architect from Dallas."

"Good to meet you, Senator Finch. I remember your parents and it sounds like you're `living up to their legacy."

"Thank you," Charlie replies, a little confused.

Lundberg takes him to meet another person a little elderly woman, no more than four foot ten.

"Senator Finch, this is Marianne Collins. She's a retired school teacher, she's a refugee but now has citizenship in Houston."

"Oh, Senator Charles Finch. It is truly an honor to meet you," she says, while shaking his hand with her cold and weak grip.

"Thank you, it's good to meet you too," Charlie replies.

"Senator Finch, this is Sharon Michelle. Sharon works for the Texas Mail Service."

"Pleased to meet you Senator Finch. The Legacy documents have shown some real potential." The beautiful woman then kisses him on the cheek. "We Texans are grateful for all you have done."

"Thank you," Charlie says. The line of people that he's introduced to continues. It includes all kinds of people, from every occupation imaginable; doctors, lawyers, gardeners, factory workers and housewives. He feels like he's meet someone from every field.

"Can I speak to you, Senator?" Charlie asks, Lundberg when he can get to him.

"Of course, excuse me."

The two men walked to an area of the room that is void of the crowd.

"What's on your mind Senator?"

"What's on yours? I'm not running for office here or anything. So why do I feel like I am? How do all these people know who I am anyway?"

"You sounded like you need some time with the common man. I could give that to you. So I did.

The common man here is a little different though. We try to encourage participation in policy, by the masses, I mean. We want those whom we serve to understand the ramifications of policy and know what is the right choice for them, not their lawmakers. This is a truly functioning system, it can work and this is the proof."

Charlie nods and looks around at all the people he met. All of them in their best clothes, they look the same for the most part. They are all treated the same here. They are all true equals here.

They all might have different opinions and backgrounds, but a sort of camaraderie has formed. No class warfare, no religious conflicts, or political sniping, just a gathering of people who understand such differences are immaterial. They have found the secret to social balance. A universal understanding of respect for each other. This is the true perfect society that the Overlord has always claimed his path would lead to.. It's here, in a place that separated from his inhumane rule of tyranny. A lack of total order creates order. Letting the people decide their own path of perfection is the only way to achieve it. The Legacy doctrine might not protect this society, but it can hinder the intrusive and corrosive influence of the Overlords or those who would follow their pathway of totalitarian rule. This is what Charlie has been fighting for, what his family sacrificed for.

This social system is so rare and precious it MUST be protected.

"Senator Lundberg, what are our chances of winning this war?"

"I don't know, pretty good. Why?"

"How can we maximize those odds?"

"Charlie, what are you getting at?"

"This is what our Legacy is. To fight against such tyrants who would destroy this country of choice.

This is the Alamo that is worth fighting for. Our chances are a lot better than they were during the war with Mexico to obtain these lands. We can hold this land again."

"What's your point?"

"Let's hit them where it hurts. A full concise calculated attack against the Empire. Bring the Overlord to his knees.

We have those outside the Capitol City on our side, a labor strike is the first step. A strike against the unions. A hit in the financial system, diverting the credits from those who enslave the citizens, back the people. We have a computer virus that does that. The resistance is the cure to all this."

"Are you talking about uniting the countries? Alaska, New Hampshire, Texas, Utah and Canada, hitting as a united front?"

"With the insurgents in the empire itself, yes. It could work. We get all their representatives here, taking them on the long trip, through the Industrial Sections. That way they see a very stark contrast. Then we work on getting their support."

"Do you think it will work?"

"Yes, I do. We have right on our side, that is the difference between the winners and losers in cases like this."

"I hope you're right.. Excuse me a moment," Lundberg says, and walks to the door that recently opened. Walking into the room is Travis and another man that Charlie has never met before. Lundberg and the other two men walk over to Charlie. When the stranger approaches he sees the man has a large scar across his eye.

"Charles Finch, this is my brother. Dragen Travis, he works in the Capitol City."

"I've heard a lot about you Senator. It's good to finally meet you. So, I understand you want to unite the countries in a common cause against the Overlord. I want you to know that I'm in. I have a certain amount of pull in the Capitol City," Dragen says, giving his brother a mischievous grin. Travis rolls his eyes and sighs in response.

"You can spread the word then, as best as you can, at least.

When Travis and I leave, we can do what we can to enlist the help of the industrial insurgents. Lundberg, can you get your fellow Texans on board?"

"That won't even be hard. Texans have always been eager to fight against tyranny."

"So, it's really just Alaska that is the challenge," Charlie laments.

"I know some people there. I'll work on them," says Dragen.

"Good. We have a plan."

"Yeah, 'Operation Finch','" Lundberg pipes in.

"What?" Charlie says, in obvious alarm.

"You know the importance of the finch?"

"You mean Charles Darwin and the Galapagos? Yes, four different finch species that developed different beaks to accommodate their dietary needs.

What does that have to do with anything?"

"Adaptability. The ability to think quickly in any given situation. Adapting and evolving to your environment, rather than having to conform to it. That is the type of soldier we need. That's the kind of militia we need," Dragen says.

"That's the kind of soldier we already have. I've been with the soldiers for the past year. Adaptable is the perfect word for them," Travis answers his brother.

"Well then, this really is perfect."

"Then to 'Operation Finch.'" Lundberg says.

"'Operation Finch,'" say Dragen and Travis in unison. They all look at Charlie, who simply shrugs and joins in. "'Operation Finch' it is."

Senator Lundberg grabs a glass off a tray that is being passed around. The others join in.

Lundberg holds up the glass. "To 'Operation Finch,'" he says. "To 'Operation Finch,'" says not just the rest of the group, but the whole room. Apparently their secret conversation is not so secret.

"Alright, so we have a name for it. What's the first move?" Charlie asks.

"Get rid of the drones," Dragen replies.

"What? Are you mad?" Senator Lundberg answers back. "I've seen what those things can do, there's no way to get rid of them."

"It's actually very possible and not a bad place to start," Charlie says. "Travis and I have shown the Industrial citizens how to make their own drones out of old cell phones. They have taken out a lot of them already. Dragen, what do you have in mind?"

"That hotel casino in Las Vegas, the new one. It's more than just a casino, it's a radio control tower. It was commissioned by the Union Leaders to commemorate Overlord Tymes. Destroy it and you kill the signal going to the domestic drones. Those need to have a nearby signal."

"The Global ones don't have to have signal towers? Why not?" Charlie asks.

"Because those are entirely unmanned. There's no reason for the Global drones to be manned. The Clergy and Military Officers are only used to keep the peace within the American borders. The Overlord doesn't want to lose them to a drone.

Overseas, however, he couldn't care less. The drones can kill everyone across the rest of the world."

CHAPTER 8

The next day the session reconvenes and the visiting dignitaries make their journeys home. Along the way Charlie, Travis and Dragen make a stop in Las Vegas to scout the building. Dragen is wearing large sunglasses everywhere he goes and tries to avoid the security cameras and drones that are all over the city. They all go inside and examine the casino more closely.

"So, what do you have in mind Dragen?" Charlie asks.

"Work on the residents here. Arm them and then they can take care of lowering the number of the soldiers within the city limits.

I'll get demolition forces in disguise to come in and while the soldiers are distracted take out the building. Or maybe use a disguised drone, make it look like one of the Overlord's. Then it will hit the building without the soldiers even getting suspicious. We'll minimize the risk of Collateral Damage by picking a day and time when renovations are being done."

"I don't know about the demolitionists but the residents are ready for a change here. I've been meeting with the citizens all the time."

"Really.. Splendid. We might make this

work yet."

The trio spend the rest of the afternoon meeting with the people there and studying the structure of the building. They figured the northern side is the best side to hit. Not only can they launch from Canada or Alaska, but it winds up being the weakest side. The union bosses must have wanted to save money and didn't properly secure that side from the elements. A wall of mold unseen by the naked eye, is making the structure prime for demolition.

Dragen has to go back to the Capitol City so he leaves after their lunch. In a public relations endeavor, Travis and Charlie request a meeting with the union bosses. They meet for drinks at one of the union bars. It's atrocious. It's dirty, unorganized and the employees are mistreated. They are less like employees and more like slaves. One of the waitresses is taken to the back of the bar by one of the union bosses. Her face is white with fear not knowing her fate. Is she going to be the victim of their legal rape or will he kill her for some manufactured infraction, that she didn't even do? A wave of anger rises in Charlie and he almost goes to intervene, but Travis holds him back.

"You know the consequences of that, Charlie. Let's save them all, not put everything at risk for one," he whispers to Charlie.

Charlie nods and sits down.

They get back to their drinks and pretend

that they don't hate the men that they are with. Many are unshaved and dirty. They look as filthy outside as they are inside. Vile twisted creatures, who treat all around them as inferiors.

Travis and Charlie get away from the inhabitants of the bars as quickly as possible. In the alley they find out what has happened to the young waitress. The shadows partially hide the broken body of the innocent being. Travis puts an arm around Charlie.

"I'm sorry. But we can't save them all," Travis reminds him.

"I know." Charlie opens his car door and turns on the automatic driver feature. He closes the door and takes off. Travis stands there for a moment watching the car fade into the distance. He looks down the alley where the dead girl lies and feels the raindrops hit his cheek. He stands there letting the weather distract him from the last couple of hours. He gets into his car and starts the journey home.

It's about noon when Charlie arrives home, he slept the entire time. It is the abrupt halt of the car that wakes him up. His family runs up to greet him and his child, predictably being the first one to reach him. He picks her up and holds her tight. Shara finally reaches him and notices he's crying. There's more going on than simply missing his family.

"Come on Brennana. Let your daddy breathe," she says, while grabbing her. "Let's come inside." Speaking more to Charlie, than her child. Eventually the dazed Charlie follows them.

"How did it go, Charlie?" Shara asks, while fixing him a cup of tea.

"The session was fine. Texas was great. It's the ideal example of what our ultimate goal is. But in America, it's gotten worse than I remembered.

The Overlord's minions are cracking down. I'm not even sure how safe a dignitary is. We met with the union bosses in Las Vegas along the way home. One of them murdered a waitress. He murdered her, he took her out back and took her life. I could have tried to stop it, but it would have been futile. I might not have come home tonight if I did, I know that. Still, I sat there, I didn't do a damn thing and sat with the ghouls that did it. I feel like a coward for it."

"You are not a coward. You are the most brave and idealist man I've ever known. That this bothers you so is proof of that. You did the right thing as far as I'm concerned. You have something bigger to accomplish, and your hands are clean. You came back to your family." After she finishes her speech, she kisses him. Sitting on the couch she guides him to a lying down position and drapes a blanket on him, and he promptly falls asleep.

Law 8 for the Tyrant:

All industry must be owned and control-led by the totalitarian state. No opposition and no exceptions, can be allowed. If left, it will thrive and the Tyrant's hold will no longer exist.

For the Tyrant, all exceptions are a can-cer, a disease that unless cured will only spread.

It takes about three weeks to manufacture their own drones, two are built in case a problem occurs. While it is being made, the resistance forces in America are breaking down the Union Officers and Military presence there. Not just in Las Vegas, but across the Industrial Sector, we-apons made from scratch are used to neutralize their immense numbers and armory.

The date for the launch is the fourth of July, at one time called 'Independence Day' it was changed by the second Overlord in his first year to the 'Overlord's Festivity Days.' A week-long celebration of the Overlords and their influ-ence and gracious will. In the resistance it is called 'Propagandus Day.'

One of the drones is moved to Alaska and the other is set to leave Canada, once set, the homing devices are activated. The signal is not picked up because it is hidden by the signal of the tower. They are completely hidden from tracking devices.

As the clock ticks down, Charlie keeps returning to the night of the Texas congress. The night that poor girl was killed. Thinking what if it had been Shara? What if it had been his little girl? She was some father's little girl.

Now the moment is closing in. Ten- Nine- Eight- Seven- Six- Five- Four- Three- Two- One- and fire! Nothing happens. The first one has malfunctioned, the message is sent to Alaska that the Canadian drone has suffered catastrophic failure.

They are given the signal to launch and they do. Moving slowly at first and then going a little faster and blending in with the other drones, the machine hovers around the building that is it's target. The targeting systems have been activated on the drone and it prepares to fire one of it's missiles. Before it can respond to the command a military drone appears and slams into it, ending the two drone's lives in a spectacular burst of fire in the sky. The explosion is already on the Ultranet and they have been monitoring their drone since it left Alaska. The drone attack has failed; now their contingency plan has to be implemented.

Charlie and Travis get changed for their mission, wearing black fatigues and hoods with eyeholes. To hide their identities further, they place scanner-proof contact lenses in their eyes.

The lenses keep retinal scanners from properly analyzing their retinal pattern. Charlie says good-bye to his family and he and Travis cross the border again.

As they make their journey through the countryside, they survey the massive changes that have taken place within a very short amount of time. The country is no longer full of compl-acent slaves. Scrimmages between the oppres-sive soldiers and the citizens are not the anomaly that it once was. The insurgents have homemade clubs, axes, knives and wooden or plastic guns. Explosives are made from cleaning products and are shattering the calm of the country. Military tanks and soldiers are all over, like swarming ins-ects they are running around attacking the citizens that are taking back the country.

It takes a couple of days to reach Las Vegas and it's in chaos, reeling from the failed attack on the casino. The travelers meet up with the resistance forces just outside of the city and are informed of the game-plan. The cas-ino is hit with a wave of insurgent forces to pave the way for Travis and Charlie as they try to get in to set an explosive device. One of the tanks has been overtaken by the resistance and the pathway is finally cleared.

Charlie makes a mad dash into the building and jumps through a partially shattered window. It takes a couple of seconds for him to recover but he looks around before getting back up.

When he does, a couple of larger pieces of glass get through his gloves and slice through his palms. He groans in pain, but gets back to his feet. The glass that he was on top of looks like painted glass from his wounds. Before proceeding with his mission he dresses the wounds. He looks around for the best place to set off the bomb and finds an ideal location near the northern corners. He's about to set a couple of time bombs, when he hears a noise in the darkness. He leaps into the shadows and hides while searching for the source.

      He sees him and he walks towards one of the bombs. The stranger bends down to examine the device and Charlie makes his move tackling him. The two scuffle on the floor and he hits Charlie in the side. Charlie head butts him and kicks him in the side. As the stranger gets Charlie on the ground, Charlie now sees the man clearly. It's the Union boss that killed the waitress. With renewed energy Charlie flips the man over top of him. He lands on his back and Charlie rushes over and hits him. He hits him again and again until he's knocked out. The bandages have started to turn red from the blows that have reopened the fresh cuts. Charlie grabs his gun and is about to shoot him, but then he puts his gun away and drags the man from the middle of the floor.

      When the stranger wakes up he finds Charlie standing over him with his mask off and a pistol in his face.

"Do you remember me?" Charlie asks. The man starts to answer, but can't because of the duct tape over his mouth. Wondering if he can move his arms and legs he tries, but finds these too are hindered. "Yes, you're tied up and gagged. Nod your head. Do you remember me?"

He shakes his head no.

"No.. I didn't expect you would. I was here a couple of weeks ago... I was passing through and was meeting with other Union bosses. How about the girl, do you remember her? Did you rape her and treat her like a whore, or just murder her? What did she do? Spill a drink on you? Tell you not to grab her? Give you a bad look? Or did you have a need to kill and she was convenient?" Charlie puts the gun closer to the man, it's now so close that he can smell the metal. The tied up man starts to cry and a pool of urine gathers under him.

"Did she cry? Did she plead with you not to kill her? You government bullies can give it, but not take it. Well, obviously tears didn't work for her and it won't work for you."

Charlie gets up, puts on his mask and sets the timers on the bombs. Getting out of the man's sight he looks outside and sees an opportunity to run. He makes a sprint that a rabbit would be hard pressed to match. Bullets flying like a swarm of bees, he manages to avoid most of the stings. He takes a shot in the shoulder and a shot to the leg that makes him trip when he reaches shelter. Behind the remains of a wall, he finds Travis.

"Well, that was invigorating," Charlie remarks to Travis.

"I'll bet. What kept you?" Travis asks.

"Nothing. Had a guard to deal with," Charlie replies.

"How did you deal with him. By tying him to the bomb?" Travis asks.

"What? No. What are you talking about?"

"Charlie! I saw you. Now what are you doing?"

"Finishing business," Charlie says.

"Charlie, we have to go get him. I don't care if he did murder some girl. This is wrong."

"Travis! No, we can't it's too late."

The explosives go off and a sound wave spreads out over Charlie, Travis and everyone in the immediate vicinity. Those standing are knocked off their feet. Then the debris from the blast hits those in the blast radius, filling the area with darkness.

Coughing and feeling disoriented, but back on their feet, Charlie and Travis take off. Those who would have seen them would have thought they were a couple of drunks.

"Alright, I think we are out of the vicinity of the blast. The soldiers won't search here," Charlie says.

"Good. Now tell me exactly what the hell you were doing? That man should have stood trial for what he did. The people should have decided his fate, not a foreigner."

"I'm not a foreigner. I'm from this country as well and escaped," Charlie challenges.

"You are from the CAPITOL CITY. Before you emancipated yourself to Canada, you knew NOTHING about what the world outside it was like.

You saw more than you should have, I'll give you that. But it was no less than what the children have had to endure their entire lives.

None of that matters though, because we are more civil than those who would perform such atrocities. How would Riddick have felt about what you did? Or your uncle? Or your parents? They would have been appalled and you know it. Even your uncle would not have done something like that."

"Alright.. Alright, you made your point. I was in the wrong."

"Okay. Then let's go home. I'm beat."

"No arguments here," Charlie says.

****

As the dust clears on the scene of carnage the Government Clean-up Agency comes through to investigate.

The officers numbered about twenty or so. They start sifting through the wreckage and counting the dead. About half of the Las Vegas Union bosses are dead, or dying. The survivors are rounded up and placed in the vans, while the investigation continues. Many are missing arms or legs. All the drones are also picked up and will later be salvaged. The fires explosives set by the insurgents are put out so the buildings can be examined.

The bodies of the civilians are put in a heap in the main square where they are burned. A couple of citizens that were hiding from the Union bosses run when they are discovered and are shot in mid stride. The Officers go up to the lifeless remains and shoot them again until their magazines are empty. The remains of the burned bodies are hung all across the city. Las Vegas is no longer immune to the Overlord's force.

The panicked remaining Union bosses turn to the officers for help.

"Let me see what we can do, alright," team leader, Crowe Sanders tells them. He gets on his radio to get instructions from his superiors. About a dozen of the Union bosses are still alive and rounded up. While he talks they have been told to wait in the vans. After a lengthy conversation the Team Leader comes back and addresses the men in the vans.

"Alright, so we have been told that we will

evacuate and move you all to the Capitol City. So sit tight and soon enough we will take you to safety."

Reassured the men in the van start to relax as the investigation is going on.

Last place they check out is the casino where the explosion took place. During their examination they discover that an accelerant was used, minimal demolition was needed because the explosives were strategically placed and neglect from the Union bosses using inferior building supplies. That is what is written in their final report at least. They examine the remains of the man that was tied to the bomb, but find nothing significant. Near one of the windows they find melted glass that looks like it was stained glass. The team leader looks more closely at it.

"Take samples of these. There was no stained glass in this place. This could be blood and I want to know if it is and whose it is," Sanders says.

The team take their samples and load up the new body they uncovered. The samples are all packed and their supplies up in one van and the Union bosses in the other three. The team leader and a few of the his team get in the same van with the Union bosses. The rest of the clean-up crew finish the job, destroying what is left of the building. As they leave the team leader watches from the side mirror as the building is turned into an inferno.

Exhausted from the anarchy of the past couple of days the Union bosses fall asleep. They are so worn out they don't even notice the other three vans don't follow the lead clean-up vehicle. They go for a couple of miles until a stop wakes the snoozing travelers.

"What's going on?" one of them asks.

"We are just stopping for a break. We will start up again in a minute. Please step out and enjoy yourselves," Sanders replies.

So all of the Union bosses get out except for a couple of them who fall back to sleep. Once they close their eyes though, something new wakes them up. The inability to breath! They find themselves with cloth rags damp from the chemicals that are flooding their systems. A couple of the officers have stayed behind and are suffocating the men left in the van. Trying futilely to vend off their attackers, they reluctantly embrace death.

The others walk a short distance up the hill and are greeted by men with guns.

"Put up your hands," says the intruders.

"What is the meaning of this?" says the Union men. The team leader and a few of the other officers also pull out guns. Union and Clean-up officers, not involved, quickly do as told; with the exception of one. The one who asked the question flat-out refuses to comply.

"The meaning of this is your execution. That's what the meaning of this is," says one of the armed men from the woods. The team leader turns to the officers with their hands raised.

"I have gotten to know you men quite well recently. You are brave and honorable soldiers. I have made a deal with the Canadian government, that if you join the resistance then we will spare your lives. Please consider this, the offer expires in twenty minutes. Let's go finish this."

The Union bosses are taken a few yards away. The soldiers aim and fire. The men slump down like rag dolls. All this is done purposely within sight of the officers, to convince them to abandon their loyalties. One of the officers bolt at this sight and is shot by a soldier. The others upon the hill run down after hearing the shot. When they reach the others the team leader questions what happened.

"He just took off. We didn't have a choice, we couldn't let him escape," he reports.

"No.. I guess not," Sanders says, with a half-smile. "Have the rest of you made your decision yet? Will you join us or join him?"

The rest of the group look at each other, unbuckle the belt where their weapons are holstered and drop them at the feet of the soldiers.

"Welcome to the resistance," Sanders says.

CHAPTER 9

"Where exactly did the Union bosses end up then?" Overlord Tymes presses his General. The man of seventy-five wrings his hands with nervous anxiety. He has been living up to the standard of the other three Overlords before him, and he hates relinquishing control. He couldn't care less the fate of the Union bosses, with them out of office his officers can employ his brutal reign in Las Vegas. He is the longest ruling Overlord and has been in office for about forty years now and is very accustomed to authority.

"We're not entirely sure yet. We have recently discovered them missing, but we don't know when their paths were diverted. The drivers were following the first unit's convoy. We should know something shortly, however," General Michaels answers.

"I hope so. This is unacceptable," he growls at his General. "How long have you been my General? Thirty years now? Thirty years, it would be a shame to end such an exemplary military career in this manner.

Whatever it takes, find them. We have to contain this."

"Of course," the General replies.

The Overlord leaves his General's chambers exasperated with his servant. Michaels walks over to the cabinet and pours himself a drink. He knows Tymes too well by now and realized long ago that he has become reliant on the General. It's kind of ironic really, knowing this man of power needs anyone but that is the reality. It's a reality that the Overlord hides very well. Without his loyal General Michaels, all this would be undone in no time. Michaels walks to the window and looks across the country, as much as can be seen at least. Even at the top floor of the Capitol City's Imperial Palace, called the 'Golden Tower' by the residents, it's difficult to see past the Capitol City's limits. Not that one would really want to. With the exception of the Northern Sector of the country, everything is charred remains and factories. The gleaming diamond in all this is the city of Las Vegas, once called 'Sin City.' It wouldn't be able to hold that title against the Capitol City.

A place where murders are not only legal, but a public spectacle. Many of the traditions that the Overlords had adopted were based on the books of ancient Rome. The days of Nero and Caligula being the most notable. For obvious reasons books about the emperors are forbidden and punishable by death. A place where rampant corruption by the political elite is heralded as the law of the land. This is the Capitol City of the New America, the land of opportunity if you're willing to sell your soul.

As Michaels sips his drink he watches the lights from the spontaneous fires spring up, like blinking stars in the night sky. He stands there and watches. Just watching, silently musing about how truly delicate this reign of power really is. On the table is a chess set, he and the Overlord play while developing strategies of attack. He walks over to it and knocks down the king piece. "Checkmate," he says, and walks back to the window.

Law 9 for the Tyrant:

The action of the Tyrant at the coming of his end will be severe. The way to combat this is to be severe in kind.

It may appear that society is breaking down, but this is not the case. This is merely the poison of Tyranny being purged, this is necessary for the healthy prosperous society to emerge.

The Overlord sends out troops to restore order in the Industrial Sectors and Las Vegas. Before their departure a gala is scheduled and the elite of the Capitol City and dignitaries of other nations are sent invitations as well. Canada and its allies are not included. Charlie and Travis are actually relieved about this, having recently pursued actions of sabotage, they were not looking forward to being back within the Overlord's realm. The dignitaries of India and China make their showing, dressed in military best. After they have been announced of their arrivals, the exotic guests are guided to their respective seats for dinner. The event lasts until late in the evening.

The troops of mixed officers, the Capitol City Branch Clergy, Military and the Overlord's Elite, his personal guards, have set out to stop the resistance. They parade through the Capitol City getting praise and adulation by the residents as they march on by. Chants of "LONG LIVE THE OVERLORD" and "DEATH TO THE TRAITORS" ring out across the city as the procession goes by. A very macabre sight in retrospection, seeing a celebration at the spectacle of a deadly force of public oppression. They wave to the crowds and blow them kisses. The hands of the closest in the audience get their hands shook. Tears of joy and gratitude are streaming down the cheeks of the crowd. Marching down the road the ground is shaking, from the weight of the thousands of men and women in uniform and the tanks following the troops. A sort of choreography with the mix of uniforms is given the same amount of careful scrutiny that the military strategies have received. The troops look like a row of fire in colors of red, yellow and orange. As they move, the wind picks up, making the effect even more elaborate and menacing.

From the 'Golden Tower' balcony the Overlord salutes their troops. The salute is made by holding up the hand the back facing the other person.

Michaels stops, faces the Overlord, returns the salute and the rest of the platoon follows his example. The tanks, similar in fashion to the twenty gun salute, fire off their cannons. The last symbols of the Overlord's empire in the Capitol City are the statues that were erected in his honor. His predecessors had their own made as well, but Tymes had them dismantled and his put in their places.

"WE WALK INTO DARKNESS FULL OF DANGER AND OF STRIFE, KNOWING NOT IF WE WILL LIVE THE NIGHT. DEFEND THE OVERLORD AT ALL COSTS, WE ARE HIS TO LEAD AND CARRY ON THROUGH ALL LOSTS. WE WILL BE VICTORIOUS FOR OUR CAUSE, NEVER TO BE BOUGHT BY OTHERS AND BE FOR NAUGHT.

WE WALK INTO DARKNESS FULL
OF DANGER AND OF STRIFE,
MAKING SURE OUR OPPOSITION
WILL END THEIR LIVES."

This is the battle song that has been engrained in them. Many of them have been in the military of some form since they were children.

As the troops continue their journey to Las Vegas they sing the song over and again, in perfect unison. Everything about the procession is in sync in fact. A showing of perfection that any dictator would be proud to call his own. Zero deviations, zero independent thought. A perfect force of war.

A few miles out a portion of the troops are separated from the rest, led by Michaels, to investigate the break in the road. This is the suspected area where the Union bosses' convoy got diverted. A couple of miles up the road they come across abandoned military vehicles. It's been a couple of days since the incident and without the drones to survey the countryside, the ineptitude of the Overlord in matters of security, is on full display. As the troops get closer to the vehicles the aroma of decay and death gets more apparent and a cloud of flies suddenly burst from the open windows, revealing a grim specter. Emaciated mummified remains of two men, both in plain black suits with once white shirts, now yellowed from exposure, typical style of the Union bosses.

"Spread out and look for further clues. The rest of the Union leaders bodies are here somewhere."

"Yes sir," say the men.

The men start exploring the open fields in the immediate area, searching through the wild long grass for any sign of a skirmish. In about an hour of searching they find a line of fired rifle shells, and twenty feet away the bodies of the rest of the Union bosses. Weathered by the elements and broken down by scavengers. Mostly they are down to only bone, tattered and torn flesh hanging from them. It looks more like spider-webbing than skin.

Michaels grabs his cell phone and dials.

"Yeah, it's Michaels. Patch me through to the Overlord. We found what's left of them. Get a couple of Clean-up teams in here."

****

Halfway to their destination, the platoon stops for the night and confiscates the homes of a the residents of the town. Most of the residents are evicted from their homes, some are assaulted and the few that stand their ground are taken out behind their homes and executed. The envoy ravage the houses, destroy heirlooms, raid their food reserves and commit other acts against humanity. But this is one of the costs of war, after all. After they have done their demolition and after breaking in to the bootleg liquor that was discovered in one of the homes, they pass out for the rest of the night.

The next day the consequences of their debauchery hangs on the bodies as the physical strain, be it a hang-over and stomach ails. Not having any sympathy for the troops self-induced torment, the lieutenant who is acting commander in Michael's absence, orders them to move with the rest of the army. By the end of the day they are to be just outside of Las Vegas city limits and setting up for the incursion, not knowing that the way to the city is blocked by the insurgents.

The local Clergy can attest to that. During one of many trips to the Industrial sectors, Charlie and Travis have been witness to a new act of in-civility perpetrated this time by the citizens. Cannibalism has come to the cities of the 'graveyard.'

A month before the drone attack on the casino, in a counteroffensive against the Clergy, the first incident occurred. The Overlord had turned off the power and water to the region, in response to a major uprising. Without basic amenities those dwelling in the Industrial Sectors have little options. Those who can hunt do so, but Wildlife is in short supply in the Industrial Sector and it is a death penalty offense within the

Northern Sector that is before the Canadian border. Those that are caught doing so are dispatched quickly and without mercy. Charlie, Travis and foreign dignitaries from Utah, assist the Industrial Sector residents as best they can, donating food, medicines and other supplies. They also keep them well armed. But they can't maintain enough for the millions of residents and many still starve to death.

Las Vegas, still being under Union rule at the time is the only city immune. Desperate for food, the mobs have resorted to eating the Clergy officers after killing them. Since then this has become a mainstream act of self-preservation.

Traps and oil-pools have been set up surrounding the area, creating a trap for the troops. This act of underestimating the enemy will prove to be fatal for the troopers and a sure victory for the starving residents of the Industrial sectors.

The confident and spirited army can see the lights of the city looming up ahead. Knowing that their Overlord is always right they are willing, and even eager, to give their lives to protect the interests of the Capitol City, its government and residents.

It took a couple of hours for the Clean-up Team and most of the work was already done. The team investigating the Union bosses mass-acre have found all the evidence they can, but those responsible are long gone. Evidence at the scene suggests they have fled to Canada and the team starts packing up.

As they get on the road a sudden explo-sion flips the first vehicle over, pinning the occu-pants in their seats. Behind them the second van, like a rocket, slams into the first. A couple of the occupants in the first are killed instantly, the others knocked out or simply injured. General Michaels still conscious, grabs his knife and cuts his safety belt. He slams hard onto the roof of the upside down van. He checks the other occ-upants, gets the ones that are alive back on their feet and pulls them out of the burning wreckage to the waiting arms of the occupants from the second van. He gets the last one out right before the fire heats the gas tank to the brink of ignition. The van explodes again. A large shard is projec-ted from the wreckage and hits into one of the survivors, impaling his lifeless body to a nearby tree.

The rest of the survivors of the first car, about seven in all, are loaded into the second. While they rest, the General and some of the others look around for the device that flipped the van. After an hour of searching they can't find anything.

"This is impossible, something has to be left. But there is no shrapnel anywhere," one of the officers gripes to Michaels.

Without notice, the officer just talking falls down dead beside Michaels. In his back Michaels sees an entry wound. Michaels grabs his pistol. Suddenly the air is filled with flying bullets. Taking down one officer after another until all but Michaels is left laying on the ground. As suddenly as it had started, the attack stops and Michaels finds himself face to face with the troop of resistance fighters.

"Sanders, do you mind telling me exactly what it is you are doing?" Michaels demands, with obvious fury.

"Freeing you General," Sanders replies. "We are part of the resistance and it is part of our job to neutralize the Overlord's force. We intend on doing just that."

"You're making a big mistake," the General replies.

"Maybe so. We'll see what Senator Finch thinks," Sanders replies.

CHAPTER 10

The remaining survivors are restrained and forcibly escorted to the back of a van a little ways from the capture point. With ruthless efficiency the troop showed the true power of the militia, cutting down a troop of twenty soldiers to five or six and destroying all the evidence that a crime was committed. That was their true intent, the soldiers simply had the bad luck of being there.

"Sir, why are we being taken to Senator Finch?" one of the officers asks Michaels.

"What do you know of the Senator?" Michaels asks.

"Not much. He's supposed to be this power-hungry politician, who wants to invade our country.

First, kill our Overlord, rape our women and take our children for his own forces."

"I've heard the same things about our Overlord, haven't you? I prefer to wait on making judgments personally," Michaels whispers back.

"Shut up back there!" says Sanders. Michaels glares at Sanders. It takes until evening to get to the town of Phoenix and Charlie's lakefront home.

"Keep on eye on them," Sanders commands.

The other men nod in compliance. Michaels watches as Sanders walks to the senator's door and rings the doorbell. While waiting Sanders looks back at the van and once the door opens turns to greet Charlie. They converse a bit and Sanders makes a gesture towards the van. Charlie walks with Sanders to the back of the vehicle where the captured officers are sitting.

"Get out of the van!" Sanders orders. The men comply, with General Michaels being the last. Charlie looks at Michaels in a moment of shock, which quickly fades.

"So this is The General Michaels. I would like to speak to him. The rest can be detained in your prison until their trials or they decide to join our forces," Charlie says.

"Lets go!" Sanders orders Michaels, pushing him with his rifle. The rest of the men are taken to the prison awaiting their own fates.

Charlie leads the men to a room off to the left side of the house. From there, Michaels is taken to a desk and pushed into a chair by Sanders.

"That will be all for now Sanders, thank you. Could you please leave us."

"Senator?"

"Just for a moment, I assure you."

Sanders nods and reluctantly does so. Closing the door tightly behind him.

"Hello, Dragen. How are things going on your end?" Charlie asks.

"As good as to be expected Senator. So I guess you are a little confused by this. General Michaels, faithful servant to the Overlord, is actually in fact Marshall Travis' brother and your deep throat."

"Now that I know.. It's not that surprising at all. How did you get captured?"

"Overlord Tymes sent me and a group of my most trusted officers to investigate the disappearance of the Union bosses. Sanders and his patrol took out the rest of my team and captured what was left. It looked like they were trying to contaminate the crime scene and we were unexpected. What did they use to blow up our van? Whatever it was, it was very effective and didn't leave anything behind."

"It was a type of EMP cannon that has been was taken from one of Tymes armories.

You should know, Dragen, that we are closer than Tymes knows to ending the war. His forces are walking into a trap, explosives and oil pools that will be ignited by remote surround the perimeter. But things are bad there. Cannibalism has even broke out in parts of the Industrial Sectors. Las Vegas is also now under the Overlord's reign."

"Well, then I better tell you that the Overlord has developed a new biological aerosol weapon; Housed in a drone, it's to be released on the city. He didn't tell me exactly what it does, but he said it was manufactured from the 2017 plague. Get your troops as many gas masks as possible, they might need them."

"Thank you, Dragen. I have a favor to ask of you and it's a large one. Shara is going to be joining me in the battle. I couldn't talk her out of it, if I'm going to die she would rather be at my side, she said. There's a good chance that both of us will be killed and we want you to take our daughter if that happens. You can get her out, I know you can. Keep her safe and after this is all over, make America what it once was, someplace special and free. Will you do this?"

"If Sanders and his troopers don't kill me first. Yes, I will."

"I'll talk to Sanders. I'll make sure nothing happens to you and that your men are treated fairly."

"Thank you, Senator. Don't worry about your child, I will treat her like she were my own. She will also know what her parents did for her."

"Thank you Dragen."

Charlie meets Sanders at the door. "Senator," Sanders greets Charlie.

"Sanders, that was excellent work today. You're definitely a credit to your profession, but we need to talk about something. First, I need to get Marshall Travis here immediately. Could you go get him? Tell him that his brother is here."

"His brother? I didn't know he had a brother."

"That's because his brother works undercover. You know him as General Michaels."

"What? General Michaels is on our side?"

"SSSHHHH!" Charlie tells Sanders. "We can't let this be public knowledge yet. Get Travis and the four of us will come up with a gameplan to end this war and the era of the Overlords forever."

After the meeting the group disperses. Travis and Sanders go down to meet with the senators in Utah to finish planning the counteroffensive in Las Vegas. Michaels goes back to the Capitol City to give the Overlord some grand manufactured scheme of how he fled the clutches of the 'Barbarians of Bedlam.' 'Bedlam,' is the recent nickname of the Industrial Sectors under siege by the revolutionaries.

Charlie heads for home, to spend the next two days with his two girls, before he and Shara leave to help with the war effort. Fishing, hiking and other typical family activities, ending with he and his wife connecting in every way a loving couple can, are the current priorities.

The next day is a continuation of the last with the three of them going to a field nearby, the ground before them is covered with the yellow flowers of spring.

Indulging in this moment Charlie and Shara are addicted to this occasion of absolute pleasure.

So rare and so intoxicating, they allow themselves to forget this may be the last hours they get to spend with their child. As are the most precious and happy moments in life sadly, it is fleeting and night falls far too soon. Out of the norm, their daughter sleeps in the same bed as them.

Charlie and Shara don't get more than a couple of hours of real sleep that night, the reality of the next day weighing on their minds.

The next day Dragen stops by to pick up the little girl, to take her stay with his wife.

Law 10 for the Tyrant:

This is the start of the decay of power. In desperation the Tyrant will react with one final blow to his opposition. This final strike to maintain his power is futile, however, and will be his undoing. It will show the cracks in his glasshouse, which has been a mirror the whole time.

The mirror that has been showing the f alse reflection of his lies, will now shine the truth. All his actions will only speed up the decay. This is the beginning of the end for our Tyrant.

The massive armada of the Overlord's force are getting closer to the Industrial Sectors and the light from the city is getting brighter. It's a ball of light that keeps getting brighter and brighter.

The troops on the march have been killing off any insurgents that have dared to face them. In a display of brute force they shoot at anything that moves, at times even committing murder since not all are armed resistance, merely innocent citizens in the wrong place. When a child is killed in the march, that does enrage the citizens to violently protest against the soldiers. Snipers hiding at the tops of the buildings wait patiently for the soldiers to get within range and take them down, causing ripple effects in the formerly perfect arrangement.

Now only feet away from the explosive charges and oil-pools setup by the resistance, the eager triggermen watch the first lines arrive. Getting more impatient and infuriated as they hear the troops. It's the battle song of the Overlord that is setting skin on edge and vexing their willpower to wait.

"WE WALK INTO DARKNESS FULL OF DANGER AND OF STRIFE, KNOWING NOT IF WE WILL LIVE THE NIGHT.
DEFEND THE OVERLORD AT ALL COSTS,
WE ARE HIS TO LEAD AND CARRY ON THROUGH ALL LOSTS.
WE WILL BE VICTORIOUS FOR OUR CAUSE,

NEVER TO BE BOUGHT BY OTHERS
AND BE FOR NAUGHT.
WE WALK INTO DARKNESS FULL
OF DANGER AND OF STRIFE,
MAKING SURE OUR OPPOSITION
WILL END THEIR LIVES."

They have been singing it for days now, even they should be getting tired of it. But they continue with the march and their battle hymn.

The first line is almost there. Now, the moment the triggermen have been waiting for… they light the oil-pools and a ring of fire spreads across the ground. Many on the front lines are immediately scorched and writhing in pain. Those closest to the origin points are already dead. Unperturbed by the sight, the soldiers behind them try to use the dead and dying as shields from the flames. Some get superficial burns but carry on. Others are completely unscathed by the fire, thanks to their fallen comrades. On they go, not letting anything deflect them from their common cause. The injured and the untouched both singing that infernal song, as they march.

Now the next wave of counteroffensives against the Overlord's army is set to begin. The explosives. With the officers approaching the triggers are pushed sending the soldiers into the air, some in whole, others in pieces. Those who can, get right back up, those who can't are stripped of ammunitions and weaponry.

On they continue, a fraction of them getting through the defenses of the rebellion forces. The number getting through is still too large for comfort for the resistance.

The first soldiers of the Overlord have now reached the people's militia themselves. Shooting, knife fighting and hand-to-hand combat are their only available options now. Many on both sides are dead or dying, the bodies are now piling up. The tanks are just making their appearance to decimate everything and anyone who gets in the way. Explosives and EMP charges are used to incapacitate the tanks. Resistance tanks from Texas and Utah come in and the Overlord's army is boxed in. More troops from Utah, Alaska, New Hampshire and Texas arrive, in the nick of time. The fight is looking up for the resistance, all they have to do is keep up their pace. By tomorrow, the fate of the country and its neighbors could be decided. But fate is rarely so kind as to leave things this way and the Empire still has one last trick.

CHAPTER 11

All across the battlefield that the city has morphed into, the winds of change for the resistance is becoming ever more obvious.

In the Capitol City the Overlord is receiving the updates of this from the soldiers in the area and the Ultranet coverage. With his reign in jeopardy he does the only thing he can do. The order to send his secret weapon is signed and a single drone is launched from the Capitol City. As soon as the sensors pick the aroma of decay from the first bodies along the way to Las Vegas, it starts releasing it cargo. From Charlie's phone comes a text message.

It reads: `The Drone on its way.` `Take needed precautions.`
Charlie signals the troops and the sirens blare. That's the signal to look for shelter and put on gas masks. As he moves for shelter Charlie trips over one of the soldier's bodies. He notices something odd on the back of the neck. The drone gets closer and Charlie moves to the body. The drone is almost over them and Charlie is almost over the body. He studies it, it looks like an.. Inoculation mark. What was the purpose of vaccinating them with the old plague serum? The

plague hasn't had an outbreak in years, yet these are recent marks only a few days old. He gets up and steps away from the dead man to look around. With the drone overhead, the soldiers don't look concerned. Why? What is this weapon? As it flies over the scene a thick fog forms, making it a blur. Everything goes quiet for Charlie as he waits to see the outcome. As quick as the silence came it ends, with a sudden series of cracking sounds. The sounds are all around like a hoard of crickets. Partially hidden by the fog, shadowy figures limp along towards the fighting mobs. The figures attack but not with guns or knives, but by leaping on people and tearing them apart. Piece by piece, they reduce the mob quickly and efficiently. The source of this new army is made clear when the cracking sounds start coming from in front of Charlie. The corpse in front of him starts moving! It gets up and turns to him, gaping as he charges   Charlie. Instinctively Charlie aims and fires. Shooting him in the head he returns him to his former state.

Shara and Travis run to Charlie and away from the area. As the trio turn to flee, they run into a tank. "Get down!" Charlie shouts, and pushes Shara and Travis to the ground. The tank fires and misses them. Instead it hits five or six zombies. Two are decapitated and the rest have their necks broken.

Flamethrowers are brought in and explosives are set to destroy the zombie hoards. Snipers start taking them out as well. The situation is well in hand and the trio's exit is not going to effect the outcome of the battle.

They have another pertinent mission to attend to in the Capitol City. They meet up with their guide in Utah and he takes them to the nearest location to a set of catacombs that were established by the earliest Americans. As the nation was expanded during the gold strikes, so too were the hidden underground passages. The trails lead from one end of the country to the other and few knew about them to begin with. The catacombs are massive structures reinforced with large columns. Inside the giant underground hole is a large train-car that is meant to get them to the entryway at the edge of the Capitol City. They sit quietly looking at the floor of the car. Charlie puts his arm around Shara and she rests her head on his shoulder. It's a three day drive that brings them to the southwest corner of the portion of the country. From here they will have to travel to the heart of the city where the Government Administration buildings are. There are three buildings and they will have to work fast to avoid security. First, they have to get there though.

The Capitol City encompasses what was New York, Pennsylvania, Massachusetts, Rhode Island, Connecticut, New Jersey, Delaware, Maryland and Washington DC, of course. Where Washington once was, is now the heart of the Capitol City. Just outside of the city they start their mission. Upon reaching their destinations reaching first they have to kill the drones and cameras. Right out in front of the first building they set an EMP bomb and run behind the nearest of the government facilities, to avoid the pressure wave that emanate from the device.

The EMP bomb goes off and knocks out all electronic devices within a two block radius. The nearby drones fall like meteors to the ground, shattering on impact. That will give them plenty of cover, the lack of coverage in the area will make the surveillance team suspicious though. So now they will have to hurry. They set the charges in the first to buildings without any problems. Two of the Administration offices are in the same complex, so setting the demolition for them, doesn't take long. Those two are set on timers to go off in fifteen minutes; the same amount of time it will take to reach the final target. On the way to the last location the Clergy forces stop them for interrogation.

"Good evening sirs, madam, how is your night going? What are you doing out here? You know that it's after curfew," says one of the officers.

"Sorry, we are from out of town. We didn't know about the curfew. We're just going home right now."

"Do you have any identification?"

"No, sorry. We left it at the hotel," Travis replied.

"I thought you said it was your home? So which is it?"

Just then the discussion is ended by the explosion of the buildings. One of the soldiers is too close to the blast and is running around in engulfed in flames. Charlie grabs his gun and opens fire, with the end result of the charred man landing in one of the buildings that was destroyed. Travis and Charlie open fire on the rest of the soldiers. Other soldiers start firing on them from around the corner. As they start to flee toward the last building they are being shot at by the clergy.

The rubble of the other buildings look like prime real estate and Travis slams the door. It's not until this moment that they notice that Shara is missing. "Where is she?"

Law 11 for the Tyrant:

The greatest tool a Tyrant has been that of complete obedience, and the only way to hold that obedience is through lies. Lies to the masses by supporters of the Tyrant and his cause.

Present the masses with absolute proof of this collision of oppressive deceit and the masses will abandon the Tyrant.

Then, you can destroy the Tyrant's glass-house.

CHAPTER 12

Charlie and Travis have to make a stand in the building. The bomb has to wait for a time now that the Clergy forces have them surrounded. They need to cut them back. They start to fire on the officers that are the only things separating them from escape. "Senator Finch! We have your wife. If you don't come out, we will execute her. Diplomatic immunity be damned. If you don't think we will, try us," says an announcer on a microphone. The next sound he hears is Shara wail in pain. "SHARA!" Charlie shouts.

"Charlie! Don't do it, save yourself," Shara replies. Charlie looks around for an opportunity to save both themselves and Shara. All the while the announcer makes further threats to the inhabitants. Charlie sees only one way out of this.

"I have an idea, Travis. But you're not going to like it," Charlie tells Travis.

He pulls out the trigger and shows Travis.

"Yeah, I don't think I'm going to like this at all," Travis replies.

The announcer has a gun against Shara's head and is starting to squeeze the trigger.

"Wait!" Charlie says to the soldier, as he

walks out hands up and open. "Where's the other one?" he asks.

"He suffered a fatal wound that finally took it's toll. He's dead."

"I don't believe you. Go in and check it out," the leader tells a couple of the other soldiers. They rush in obediently. As they search the dark, they see a body on the ground, it's burned beyond recognition. "We found a body and it looks like the other one. It's burned really bad though," reports one of the soldiers to the team leader, via radio.

"Alright, come on back," the team leader tells them. "Senator Finch, we are taking you back to base.

"Team load up," the team leader orders. Suddenly the building erupts in a wall of fire, spitting out the completely burned bodies of the soldiers who went in, also knocking everyone else off their feet. This gives Charlie time to act and he goes for Shara, together again they hold the team leader hostage.

Travis then walks out from around the building, using the charred wall from the already burned building to make himself look like a burned victim. His work of camouflage has saved them. That's when the other soldiers that had been hiding surround them.

"I'll kill him. I swear I will. Back up!" Charlie threatens.

"We'll save you the trouble," says the

closest soldier, and shoots the team leader in the head.

"The Overlord's the only important one. Anyone else is expendable," the shooter replies.

"That's got to make you feel good," Charlie answers back. Using the dead soldier as a shield, Travis and Charlie start shooting as they seek shelter from them. Along the way Travis is shot and killed. Charlie and Shara see a vehicle, but it's about twenty feet away, a long distance at this moment. They make a mad dash for the car and Charlie too is shot. He falls to the ground.

Next thing, he sees himself in a foggy, unfamiliar place. It's a green valley and as it starts to clear he sees a small group of people walking towards him. It's his parents and uncle.

"Charlie," says his mom.

"Mom? Is that really you? Where am I?" he asks her.

"It's kind of a waiting area. Somewhere between the world of the living and the afterlife."

"You mean, I'm dead?" he asks.

"Not entirely. You still have more to do, my son."

"Why? Haven't I done enough? I'm so very tired... Can't I just stay here with all of you? Where there's no more pain, anger, or fear?"

"I'm sorry. But no, Shara is still there and she needs you now." Charlie hadn't considered that and looks down. "You have to finish this.

It's your cause."

"You mean like fate? You know I don't believe in fate. I decide what happens to me."

"Not fate, as much as faith."

"I don't know that I have that either," Charlie replies, feeling defeated.

"I'm not talking about religious dogma. I'm talking about the faith of doing something because it is right. That is the faith of humanity and you don't need to be a theologian to possess that. You just have to try to do what is right."

"We're very proud of you Charlie," his dad chimes in.

"You have to go back, for now anyway," his mom says again. They start to blur and their voices muffle. The last discernable words Charlie hears are, "I love you, my son." He can't tell which of his parents said it though.

He wakes up in a cold dark cell, somewhere he doesn't know. He can hear that he's not alone and calls out. "Who's there?"

"Charlie, you're still alive? I'm so relieved," says the disembodied voice of Shara.

"Shara, where are we?"

"In the Capitol City's government building. I think this is the Justice Department's center."

Almost on cue, a officer comes in and approaches Charlie's cell. "Senator Finch, You have been called to report to the Head of the Justice Department. Now that you are awake, that is."

"What if I resist?"

"Then we have been told to break your legs and drag you there," he replies.

"Well, then I'll go without a fuss."

A hood is placed over his head and he's led to a dimly lit room. He hears the door open, a couple of men enter the room and sit down. From behind him he feels the hood pulled off.

"Well, Senator. I've been waiting to meet you since I found out who you really are," says one of the men.

"Since you found out who I am? Who am I?" he replies with indignation.

"Come now. Look where you are. You can stop pretending. We know who your parents were, your father the well-respected Senator Thayer and his wife. Executed for treason ten years ago. Does this sound familiar?"

"Oh, so that's it. You have the wrong man."

The guard behind him hits him hard in the back of the head.

"You can talk all you want, Mr. Thayer.. Your genes don't lie. We tested your blood while you were knocked out. The sample was also tested with another sample gathered at the scene of the casino bombing, it proves you are guilty there too. We have it confirmed all this, so you might as well cooperate with us."

"Will Shara and I get to live if we cooperate?" Charlie asks.

"No of course, not."

"Then I think I'll keep my mouth shut."

"I'm sorry to hear that," says the interrogator, who slams a hammer on the table right where Charlie's left hand rests. Charlie howls and winces in pain at the blow. He moves his hand and feels the dead weight of the broken digit.

"Will you talk now?"

"Never," Charlie growls back.

The interrogator's response is the same as the first and Charlie loses the use of a second finger.

For the next two weeks, he is brought in for interrogations, without a pause in his resolve he doesn't tell them anything. At the end of the sessions his left hand is completely broken and his face has burn scars from the interrogator cutting his face with heated knives.

At the end of the last session, he is told he and Shara will be executed. The next month he is left in his cell.

As Charlie waits for his execution, he contemplates everything that has happened to get him here.

The agony of becoming orphaned while still a child. Seeing all his family members' deaths. Learning about how to fight, how to survive. The reason for all this.. a book. That book, Legacy. At times he cherished it and other times he hated it. But if not for that book he might not have known Shara. That is a completely different kind of hell he doesn't want to think about. She's in a cell about ten feet away. That is the greatest agony right now, being so close, yet... So far.

She is silent as well, wondering what it will be like. Is there an afterlife? Will she see her mother again? The most precious thought she has though, no more pain. In death they will know more freedom than they did in life.

In the Overlord's military chambers, Overlord Tymes is in counsel with his most trusted adviser, General Michaels. "Your Excellency, I must object to giving Charles Finch and that woman a political execution. A common-man one is the best way to go.

If we behead him, or bring in a firing squad, it will only empower his movement. It will embolden his followers into anarchy. The resistance has already made it's way into the Capitol City, thanks to this barbarian and the defectors here."

"What have you done about those defectors, since you mention it?"

"We have been rounding up those we have reason to believe are guilty of treason. They will be executed after intense interrogation."

"Good. As for today's execution, you might be right. I'm nothing if not a cautious man. Yes, hang them. Finch and his woman will be dead on the noose in five hours time. Make it happen."

"Yes, your Excellency." The General salutes and leaves the room.

He goes down to see the prisoners. "On your feet Finch," says the prison guard.

"Now, that's not necessary. He's already been sentenced to death, because of treason."

"When?" Charlie asks.

"Five hours from now," Michaels replies.

"You know what my one regret is? That I didn't get enough done. That there will still be so many here in the Capitol City that are under this monarch's spell. If the residents could only see the truth with their own eyes."

"Well maybe that's not your weight to bear," Michaels says before exiting.

Charlie walks away from the doorway and sits down on the bed.

In due time, Micheals comes back down. "It's time," he tells the condemned. The guards open the doors and shackle first Charlie and then Shara. Then the guards take their positions behind the prisoners. They are led to the first doorway and wait while one of the guards opens the security door. From there, they are led down a hallway adorned with different portraits of the Overlords and their families.

"Being rewarded for being the most ruthless.. That's what their Legacy is in the end. You have to kill your brother to become the next Overlord. What a world, eh boys," the General says to the guards. The guards just chuckle at these remarks.

The last of the doors are opened and Charlie and Shara are greeted by the bright lights of the spotlights and the roar of anger and hate for them by the audience. Going from the dimly lit and silent hallway to this, is painful in of itself. Charlie and Shara are led to the stage, with the spotlight following them all the way. From the crowd they can hear them start the routine chant.

"LONG LIVE THE OVERLORD! DEATH TO THE TRAITORS!"

They reach the stage and the nooses are wrapped around their necks. It's a very coarse material is the first thought Charlie has, the second is of Shara. He looks over at her and she at him. They ready themselves for the inevitable.

Then a loud boom echoes across the arena and on the all monitors, showing the scenes from the Industrial Sector. The Clergy and the other military guards of the Overlord, tormenting the citizens. Guards coldly, executing innocent men and women, at times in front of their children. The killing of the family in Las Vegas that started the war. It was men in Clergy uniforms that clearly did it. Meetings with the Union bosses, Industrial bosses, and the Overlord. All the dirty secrets of the Overlord and his cohorts are exp-osed to the Capitol City residents and even the government run media can't hide it now.

Not looking away from each other, tears of joy fill the couple's eyes. They have done it, the Capitol City inhabitants have seen the unad-ulterated truth. "RESISTANCE," Charlie and

Shara, both yell at the same time. Stopping only because the Overlord orders the execution for them right then. Both die immediately, with only twitches from the last firing of nerves causing movements from their bodies. For a couple of minutes there's only silence. As cold and dark as the night is surrounding those attending the event.

Then one person speaks.

"LONG LIVE THE HEROES! DEATH TO THE TYRANT!"

Then another member of the crowd joins in,

"LONG LIVE THE DEAD! DEATH TO THE TYRANT TYMES!"

Another chimes in, and another, and another, until within minutes the whole audience is chanting for the Overlord's demise.

In his theater box the Overlord and his assistants, step back before the crowd gets too out of hand. He heads downstairs to exit the arena, but once the doors are open a group of the audience has already found its way to them. His aides are swarmed and attacked by the crowd. They are about to descend on Overlord Tymes, when a bunch of the guards in riot gear show up and fire gas canisters in the crowd. Coughing from the gas the Overlord is carried away from the attackers.

"Where have you been? I will have to speak to the General about your slow reactions. I am to be protected at all times."

The guards pause and secure the door. The men take off their helmets and all pull out pistols.

"Hey, what do you think you're doing? You can't have guns within the Capitol City, let alone point them at your Overlord?"

"Shut up, Tymes! You're not in charge anymore!" snaps one of the men. The rest nod in agreement, smiling maliciously at their prisoner.

"Do you even know who we are?" another of the men asks him.

"No.. Who are you?" Tymes asks.

"I'm Team Leader Crowe Sanders and we are the defectors that were going to be executed," he answers.

"Oh no.. No. . NO!" Tymes exclaims, while trying desperately to flee from this new threat. As expected, they start to chase him, like any other predator chasing it's prey. He follows the same hallway that the condemned walked through only moments ago. The once familiar and comforting pictures of family and his predecessors now haunt him, taunting him at every turn.

Finally he finds a reprieve, with an unlocked door. He opens it, finding General Michaels sitting at the desk in the middle of the room.

Resting on the desk is a pistol and a piece of paper.

"MICHAELS! Thankfully it's you. Your men have lost their minds. They are hunting me down like some kind of a beast! You have to help me!"

"You don't have to worry about them. They won't come in here, I instructed them to leave us alone. They are quite sane, Tymes, and only following my orders."

"What? What is going on, General?" Tymes shouts, confused by what is happening around him and his lack of ability to do anything about it.

"This is the end of the war, Tymes. The time of the Overlords is ending as well, you will see to that."

"What do you mean?" Tymes says, with sudden fury.

"Because you're going to kill yourself, or we are going to show you get killed by your own troops. Either way, you're going to be gone and the country will know about it. My men are outside and if you try to flee again, they will kill you. The choice is yours."

"Why are you doing this, Dragen?" Tymes pleads.

"Why? WHY? Because you are without a doubt the meanest, most vile creature, I have ever met. You enslave a nation. Kill millions of innocent people, most being your own citizens no less. Successfully performing a genocide on the Caucasian men in America, killing off every last one. Started wars with our neighbors and put our national security in jeopardy, and all for

WHAT? To increase your already strong grip on your slave nation.

Why am I doing this to you? Because this is what you and yours' have been doing to this country for the last fifty years.

My real name is Dragen Michaels Travis and my brother was Sergeant Marshall Travis, one of many victims in your last incursion.

Another victim of the Era of the Overlords was our parents, Valerie and Dragen Michaels Senior. They were attacked and killed when we were children. I was seven and it was during the time of the Second Overlord. After Marshall and I were adopted, I joined the Military Youth in hopes that one day I could bring the Overlords down. My parents were good honorable people and were killed for speaking out. My brother never knew them. He was the last fatality in the war with Canada and its allies.

It seems like Charlie Finch slipping through the cracks of the identity system isn't so odd an occurrence. My brother and I got through and if it had worked you wouldn't have executed your own daughter. Finch's wife, you see, was the bastard seed of one of your periodical raping parties you so loved. You had her mother killed the night she was found. All this is not an endorsement on the efficiency of government, but then again, government has never been all that efficient.

This horrible act against you, is in fact

mercy I'm giving you. Which is more than you deserve. Read the paper first, it's very enlightening."

With that last statement Michaels walks out of the room, to let Tymes decide his fate.

Looking at the desk, with a shaking hand Tymes grabs the pistol and note with one hand. He sets the pistol down and opens the note. It reads:

Law 12 for the Tyrant,
This is the final law for the Tyrant, one that should make his blood run cold. The end result for the tyrant is always the same. A nation in ruins and   the death of the Tyrant.
The only way to completely kill his Legacy is his demise being in secret, preferably by his own hands. The blood of the guilty on the hands of the innocent is hard to wash away completely. Even if not seen, the stain may still remain.

He puts the note down sweat and tears running down his face. He sees the shine from the pistol and with the weight of the situation on him, he reaches for it. The apparatus of his demise seems very heavy in his hand, but with a shaking hand he puts it in his mouth and closes his eyes.

The soldiers are still outside his room waiting patiently for Tymes to make his decision.

"General, permission to speak freely," Sanders requests.

"What is it, Sanders?" Michaels asks.

"Why are we doing it this way, sir? Why not just execute him outright? Or give him to the citizens to take care of?"

Right before the General can answer, a pop is heard from inside the other room.

"Check him," Michaels instructs a couple of the other soldiers.
They look in and come out, turning to the General they nod their heads.

"Good, it's done. As for your question soldier, I don't want the impetuous and angry mob to commit actions they might later regret. It's hard to kill the monster without becoming one yourself.

I want for us not to wonder about our actions today. I want future generations to look at what we did here and not wonder about our actions as well. We could have killed him, but would we be better men for it? What many don't ponder, is the implications of what their Legacy will be. Ask yourself- Will our children forgive us?"

THE END

COMMENTS

Some will comment about this book, saying that it's covering very controversial topics and being offended by the very mention of the subjects. That is not my intention, the act of offending just for the sake of offending. Although I do have a fair amount of respect for those who do, this is an excellent form of marketing and does help bring up taboo topics for debate.

The fact is my reason for delving into such distasteful concepts is because the very idea of a totalitarian regime is far more offensive than anything I discussed here. The idea of totalitarianism is the very act of raping the civilized world and should be opposed at every opportunity.

Instead thanks to our pop culture elite, that turns athletes and actors into demigods over those advocates of real substance. Because of them, we as a collective culture, view political ideologies such as socialism and communism as simply 'misunderstood.'

Many other authors have covered these dictatorship regimes in their books. I don't think many have pushed the envelope as much as this or used such real life patterns in their story. This is a fictional book, and no, I don't necessarily believe this is the ultimate outcome. I don't believe in absolute outcomes, for one thing. If one does intervene in an event the outcome could be altered.

This book is about taking myths and conspiracies from pop culture and bringing them into on entirely plausible future.

There are things that I didn't go into much detail, but that some readers might be curious about. I'm going to address what my perceived concerns now.

How did this happen?

This probably tops the list. Well it starts with the events that are in place right now. After winning his third (and illegal) tem as president, he gets further involved with the same crony capitalist elements and extremists he has always consorted with. Making promise after promise that he in the end can't keep and trying to keep calm those who he owes.

One of these groups has finally had it and the assassination plot is made. It's an old one and not the first time it has been enacted, this time is different though. This time it works. Kill the president, the Vice President and the Secretary of State. The three heads of power are severed. Now what?

Well, this is where John Wilkes Booth and Lee Harvey Oswald, got it wrong. Even if their plan had worked they didn't plan ahead. The out come for the South under Andrew Johnson is evidence of that. Anyway, after the death of the president, Martial Law across the nation is implemented and the extremists take over the government. This is the first Overlord. He gets killed after only a couple of years. The second one also has a short reign. The third lasts for about ten years and he is killed by the fourth one, Tymes who is in charge in this book. Tymes is considered by many to be the most ruthless and inhumane of all of them, which since his reign is for forty years makes a lot of sense really.

Why is the story so violent?

Anyone who read my other writings, especially my other book, *'We the Rodents'* will be in for a shock with this story. In comparison with my other work this is very violent. Where's the whimsy and humor that is fairly trademark with my usual work? Well, I had a different intention with this book.

Realism to the subject, for the most part. These political systems are ones of control and force. Physical, psychological and emotional manipulation are tools of the trade of the authoritarian.

That's also why the characters are so emotional in it. The showing of pleasure and pain. Unbridled joy or the torturous sting of grief. All the good that comes their way ends up dashed to bits by the authority figures.

All the while others who are enamored by the dictator and are blind to the real suffering they and those around them have to endure. They, like everyone else will quickly turn on their oppressor, however, once they see the truth.

How come there are guns in the story if they are outlawed?

They are not outlawed entirely. Only certain military forces can have them and that's only during specific 'State of Emergency' situations. The citizens are not allowed to have firearms though.

More than that the very action of self-preservation has been outlawed. I've been called paranoid on this speculation, but the evidence does point this way to me.

First, take away the non-sporting guns, then the hand guns, then the hunting guns, then knives and blades, and lastly all forms of hand-to-hand combat are illegal. The gun owners rights are obviously under attack and hand to hand already has some legal restrictions. But in order for there to be a society described in the book, all forms of self defensive cannot exist. The military and police have to be the only defense for the citizens.

The main characters are not married, they're atheists and one of the military groups is called 'The Clergy.'

Are these anti-Christian overtones?

Not at all (even though I'm sure I'll get accused of that).

Charlie and Shara are not married because they are atheists first off, but also because in the America of the future all marriages have to be granted by the government. Otherwise it's considered null and void and the couple could face prosecution by the overzealous 'Department of Ethics and Virtues.'

A government agency that penalizes those who don't conform to the norm of the Overlord in power. Everything is regulated down to how many children you have and if you can even have children to begin with. From there it depends on the needs of society which gender you can have. If the need changes before the child is thirteen and placed in their occupation the child is euthanized. The fears from living under this system convinced Charlie and Shara not to marry.

The atheist theme is not a criticism of Christianity, but the power of the anti-religious utopian dream. In their minds no religion equates no religious squabbles. I'm really making a comment about that.

After *Hurricane Katrina* there was a group

of local first responders called the Clergy. They have taken the progressive, ethical apathetic philosophy, and intertwined with religious dogma. To make a community outreach group with the most tyrannical agenda. When they came to the houses of the victims rather than aid them, instead they illegally confiscated their firearms. The reason that locals are used in this agency is because the other residents trust them and that makes them more compliant. In the future this relationship is abused to whole new levels.

What's with the cannibalism and zombies towards the end?

The cannibalism, while considered downright gruesome, is a reminder of our will to survive.

It's a comment from incidences like the *Donner Party* and other such extreme moments of survival. When the power and other utilities are shut off in the Industrial Sector the residents have to turn to extremes to survive.

Even more this is the manufactured desperation that the dictator will try to capitalize on. Make them fully dependant on the system and punish them when they try to deviate from that dependency.

The zombies have both a literal and a figureative purpose in the story.

The figurative is fairly obvious. Those who

are part of the system will follow with complete surrender of their own freewill.

Before writing this book I also came across an epidemic of humans near-death, in a zombie-like trance. It was during the black plague and it was believed to be from a mutated variant of the plague that caused the condition.

William Shakespeare was an observer to it and it was said that after witnessing it his plays changed from light-hearted to the tragedies with supernatural players that were common in his later works.

*Why the Darwin themes?

Originally it was only supposed to be a comment that the adaptability in capitalism is absent in such totalitarian regimes. But it grew into something bigger to the connection with the main character.

After his parents and uncle's deaths, the child needed something inspiring. While insightful and provocative because of its illegal status the book LEGACY he finds in the story doesn't fill that need. So he keeps reading. He comes across the studies of Charles Darwin. The discussions about how these finches have to alter themselves to survive their environment hits home.

Charlie's need for adaptability is emotional and psychological, not biological, but the lesson still helps the child deal with a situation that he is not ready for.

Another theme in this book has to do with the formation of niches in political or social systems.

The first example of this, is not actually in the story itself, but has to do with how the Overlords first came to power. After the death of the president and his staff, the perpetrators created a niche to take advantage of.

Another example, is how Canada becomes a super-power in the story. With the downfall of the United States, a niche for a capitalist society occurs Canada and England are the most likely to fill it.

Do you (the author) have a fear or contempt of the police or other authority figures?

Only politicians, police or military who over step their authority.

There are police who are good, honest and help people. They are also the ones who follow the letter of the law. There is a attitude that has spread that the police should be allowed to side-step the law in their enforcement of it. This is beyond ridiculous! They, before ANY should be held to the strict standard of complete adherence to the law.

Because of the way the system is implemented, and the stressfulness that comes from their occupation, it favors the police. That is why it is important to hold them to a higher standard.

The philosophy of non-repercussions for officers who violate their oaths to 'Protect and Serve' is the norm and is having the unintended consequences of legitimizing their bad behaviors. The incentives for good behavior are simply not there.

I'm not blaming the police for this, but those who created this system of non-compliance with legal statutes.

What exactly is the LEGACY?

The LEGACY is the intention of the leader of the country. Does he want to be remembered as a inhuman monster, destroying all the rights of the citizens or be a benevolent and gracious leader.

Many of the United States presidents have been given a pass on their actions against the people because history will vindicate them.

All because they were dealt a tough hand, or overcame enormous obstacles to get where they are. This philosophy is destructive to the man in charge and to the people. Neither benefit from it and it hinders his potential to be a good leader.

If they make their decisions based on the simple thought of how will I be remembered, would they make different choices? This is important for them and the people to consider because a state of emergency is not an adequate justification for the stripping of the people's rights.

If no other lesson is taken from this story and hope that this is it.

POP-TOPIA

This is an Essay inspired by the book. It's a critique of our quest for perfection and how it makes us vulnerable to the influences of those who wish to enslave us.

Fake breasts, fake eyelashes and pretty much another part of the human body are altered with surgery. Corsets, neck extensions, high healed shoes and other such garments are used to create the perfect version that we could be. Botox injections, using an extremely dangerous toxin for the vain purpose of getting rid of wrinkles.

This of the pursuit of perfection, the quest for the modern pop culture version of the Utopian state. Utopia is a conception that many have misunderstood and if they really understood it they wouldn't equate it with a type of paradise, but the prison that it is. Those who advocate such an idea don't understand that Utopia is a country devoid of diversity. No contention, because individuality has been abolished. Not many would really consider this to a positive, unless they plan to take advantage of it.

The first major stumbling block with concern to the Social Utopia implementation, is that it is quite impossible. The perfect society is subjective and different for all. So as we can see it's very creation is fraught with problems.

The worst thing about all this, is the extreme variations within this pursuit. The most destructive lifestyles get turned into acceptable everyday practices in society.

Teeth whiting, with the eagerness to get the product out to the market it won't be surprising to hear reports in twenty years that it causes some form of cancer. I've never looked at an attractive woman and thought, if only she had a whiter smile, anyway.

The Heroin Chic look, as it has been referred, the advocacy of the dangerous practice of anorexia.

When *Sports Illustrated* model Kate Upton first started with the magazine she was called "full-figured" by one of these organizations.

Jennifer Lawrence, star of *The Hunger Games*, received similar criticism. In a tweet she stated that according to Hollywood standards she would be considered overweight.

Also on this list is the already self-conscious and extremely attractive, Jennifer Love Hewitt.

This is beyond disturbing when someone of their proper, healthy weight is berated by a group of simpletons with a twisted idea of beauty. This is even worse though because this is an active assault being launched by an organization, bent on making sure that such a self-destructive form of pretentiousness is put before a women's health. When did we get to the point that looking like a Holocaust victim is considered desirable? The number of victims of the weight loss conspiracy is unending. Brittany Murphy died because of the side effects of a weight loss supplement.

Here's a hint for those considering losing weight, consult a doctor first. Don't consult Cosmo.

This call for perfection often times is the nothing short of abandoning commonsense. I'm making a plea for commonsense, don't contribute to this epidemic of superficiality.

To the ladies out there, let's stop the catty behavior and contentious furor of criticizing others of your gender for petty grievances.

It's harmful to society and to your gender.

To everyone, though, I would say let your imperfections stay distinctions and not a focal point to obsess about. If it's not a health risk, let it go.

Through these actions, the slow process of turning us from richly distinct individuals into human Barbie dolls is being achieved.

Superficial, submissive, mindless beings without any real consciousness.

Real life Zombies. That is the goal of those in power, to turn the masses into a hoard of unified beasts of burden. That only covers a small part of Pop Culture Utopia, the fraction that is rampant in the glamour and beauty crowd. This doesn't even start to cover the full scope of manipulation that is in the American culture.

In 2008 the showing of Pop Culture's reign in the realm of politics was brought out into the open. With the presidential campaign between John McCain and Barack Obama.

Not only because of the end result was get ting Obama elected, but the entire campaign was a showing of absurdity in our political system. It left many disenchanted with politics and I do contest that it had a factor in Obama's reelection.

The damage done to the party by the RINO's like John McCain, Newt Gingrich, John Boehner and others are a showing of the hypocrisy that has become an epidemic in the GOP. It shows that neither side are not concerned with legal statutes and constitutional purity. That has become a vulnerability of these people. It has also created vulnerability for the respective party, because a culture of extreme paranoia has festered throughout the nation.

Mistrust of the government and it's representatives is healthy and prudent, but an attitude of fear towards them shows that we are far from where we as a nation need to be. This is the Pop Culture Utopia in politics in action. This is akin to socialism or communism, or some other unnamed kind of totalitarian system.

Both sides try to place full responsibility on the other for this corrosion, but the truth is both have blood on their hands in this. Establishment Republicans are just as much a threat, as establishment Democrats, neither are looking out for the country but instead their own careers.

Another part of this is the abandonment of logic when it comes to their statements concerning civil rights. Again this is an issue on both sides.

Vice President Joe Biden, has been reported saying "The average American doesn't care about Civil Rights." What a small opinion Biden has about the American people.

Lindsey Graham and John McCain have been downright hostile to anyone who addresses concerns about the breakdown of the second amendment and privacy rights. Lindsey Graham stated, the question (did the president overstep his authority in concern to drones in the United States) was offensive. Offensive, senator? The right to privacy and restrictive government is offensive? I find the fact we have to have the debate offensive.

Another example of pop culture utopia in action is the two party system's establishment attitudes toward the other parties.

Ann Coulter made an appearance on Stossel and made statements condemning libertarians for their endeavors in putting the need for change in social issues before economic sanity. Her false analysis was that libertarians only focus on the social issues while avoiding economic downfalls. Those who follow the discussions in the libertarians circles know that's not true.

Coulter has basically been antagonizing those not without any contention towards (in a few cases even in agreement) some of her opinions for no reason. She had believed false rhetoric and didn't have all the information.

Bill Maher, who has in the past been quite civil to the libertarian party, also joined the ranks to condemn the movement. He felt that he was "betrayed" by the representatives. Believing that they want the government to legalize everything and not understanding the true premise of the movement- getting government out of the everyday lives of it's citizens. This is very Pop Culture and very wrong.

Another recent trend in the world of 'Poptopia' is the new emergence of Virtual Currency.

The company that has started this, introduced the world to something called bit-coins. This is a leap forward in the dangerous prospect of Globalization and the Global Economy. Why is this bad?

Because first off it eliminates countries individuality. That is a form of soft force conformity, making the people easier to control. Secondly, it makes the economy easier to control, but on a global scale. Look at the problems that have sprung up from the EU. If one country goes down, they all go down. There's no place to turn when such tribulations arise. The Global Economy is not only inefficient but dangerous.

As I stated earlier, pop culture Utopia is one of deviance from commonsense. The reemergence of commonsense is the key to fixing this.

Related articles

These are a few articles from my blog *americanuslibertae.wordpress.com.*

The subjects discussed ties into the book, *LEGACY,* so that's why it's included.

SECESSFUL

Over two hundred years ago the threat of secession was looming over this country. A time bomb, that almost killed the American Experiment in it's infancy. Now this has become an topic for debate in modern times once again.

There are parts of the situation that when brought to light may make people rethink their positions on the matter and even consider this action as justifiable.

First off, the constitutionality is not as clear cut as the proposals critics make it sound. There is arguably sustainable points in the tenth amendment.

If the states have gotten to the point of considering dissolving the union, than the argument could be made that the president has become a tyrant, breaking his contract with the people.

Second, the numbers of people reported supporting it are not as low as critics say. When first reported it was a small portion of only about 20 states, give or take. *The Blaze. com* reported the number of states in favor at 47.

Included in the list are many blue states, parts of the eastern seaboard and California among them. I will say that cynicism of critics within that demographic does have some validity, I agree.

In states like Utah, Alaska, or Texas on the other hand, this should be deemed as serious and needing of a response by the president.

One possible reason for a low response number for secession could be that much of the media doesn't want to make Obama look bad, so they won't report the circumstances unless it escalates out of control. Look how long it took the mainstream media to report on the Benghazi attack.

Lastly, in the end it doesn't really matter the concluding results of the endeavor are really. This is less about making this prospect a reality, as much as making a bold statement to the totalitarian-leaning administration of power.

The leader of the Texas Nationalist Movement was on *Hannity* and said as much. Saying in the end this is basically just asking the president for permission to secede.

Revolution, peaceful or not, is at times needed to remind those who believe they are in power, who's really in charge. The People. For far too long the people have been satisfied with the dominant status quo, now they are saying- No More. I have made the statement on the *Politically Social* webpage, saying I would sign such a petition not just supporting them, but joining them if it comes to that. I stand by those remarks and would not hesitate in making my actions match my words.

Our founding fathers were willing to put

everything on the line by signing a piece of paper-
the Declaration of Independence. If called to do
the same thing today wouldn't you if needs be?
What if this is our call to action?

CHAOS THEORY REVISITED

In the 1960's the scientific community came up with a revolutionary new theory that endeavored to explain the anomalies that occurred in social and scientific theories.

The end result they called Chaos Theory.

The main example used that was its very backbone, was when a butterfly flaps its wings, in say Florida, and a Tsunami in Japan is the outcome. It's actually still an unpredictable result basically.

The real problem I've observed isn't that they were wrong with the theory, just it's incomplete.

This theorem only explains the anomaly's existence, not the most important and insidious part of the formula. The Implementation Phase.

This is where the term "State of Emergency" comes into play.

The implemented "State of Emergency" scenario is as follows:

First, the anomaly occurs, then the populace calls for actions from their representatives, and lastly, the representatives act. The end result is almost always the same, however, that we end up forfeiting one of our liberties for a feeling of false security. The sad thing here is that we are not learning this lesson.

All over the world, through out history, those of authority have used this tactic for millennia. But our presidents have had to be very creative in their manner of implementation. Woodrow Wilson and Franklin Delano Roosevelt, are a couple of prime examples of the abuse of power in this scenario. They sent many of our troops to war after the actions of political malice, through terrorist acts that were inflicted against us. Understand I'm not questioning whether or not entering the World Wars was right or not, but whether or not their methods of entering it were morally justified, or if their conduct during it was the right course of action.

Many speculate FDR let the attack on Pearl Harbor happen because he was anxious to enter the war effort, some have the same feeling about Wilson. I'm in that demographic, War is a big money machine and both men had large appetites. This isn't the end of abuses done by Roosevelt though. In an act of pacification to calm the people, the president had concentration camps built in America for it's citizens of German and Japanese lineage.

This would not be the last time concentration camps would be utilized in the U.S., though. Let's not forget the FEMA camps set up after Katrina, or the abandonment of the second amendment in the areas during the crisis.

Even more egregious, under this "State of

Emergency", Martial Law drills were performed in select cities across the nation. But we can't forget about the Patriot Act, this era's national version of Watergate (the policy, not the scandal).

Now onto our current administration's misuse of power.

The Bailouts for one, using it's citizens own tax money to buy the Automotive, Housing and Financial interests out from under them. Supporters of the president and his decisions, would argue, that he had to do it that if he hadn't we would have lost these industries. That's not even close to the truth.

If they had been left to work it out, they would have been forced to "cut the fat" and the unhealthy cancerous growths on these structures would have been removed. With bankruptcy comes a stronger, healthier company, ready to compete with the big boys again.

Now on to the TSA, the attempts by terrorists to bomb our planes. What shall we do? I know, treat everyone as though they are terrorists, and let a bunch of random strangers grope women, seniors and children. If they refuse, how about sending them through a huge X-ray machine. Lets ignore our personal liberties and rights of privacy for a feeling a security, performing policies that in the end will prove fruitless to their intended purpose.

Fact is, if the terrorists are that determined to kill us, they will find ways taking advantage of the weak spots we don't know about. Remember too, if we change our behavior in response to an attack, the terrorists win.

Now onto the Newtown shooting. The actions of the president when this first happened was right, to give him due credit. He addressed the nation, giving a heartfelt speech of condolences to the victims families. Other members of his party, on the other hand, were not so cordial. Many were demanding action, in the form of more restrictive gun control. Now that the dust has settled, he has joined the bandwagon, praising the U.N. official policy on gun rights. Basically no rights, what-so-ever.

The supposed party of opposition is just as wrong on this issue, asking to make our schools fortresses. Arm and empower the teachers, not bring in the S.S. Or better yet, lets find out what really caused this tragedy and not jump to the conclusion that a uniform or impetuous solution is the best one. Find out what the warning signs were that were missed, so these events can be neutralized.

Recently we had the "fiscal cliff" agreement, that was neither a compromise, nor beneficial. Out of any options that were put on the negotiating table, the best was going off the "fiscal cliff." True, everyone's taxes would have gone up, but we would have gotten mandatory spending cuts out of the deal.

Besides, the dirty little secret is that all taxes will go up anyway with the full implementation of Obama-care.

In conclusion, there is a solution to this problem, and a very simple and powerful one. The people, you and I. We can make sure that our liberties are not eroded, or traded for services that the public will never see. But we need to let cooler heads prevail. Let the facts be uncovered and don't ask for immediate action. This may sound like a lot to ask for some, but patience is how we solve such problems, not with pointless impulsive action. Careful analysis, reflection and debate, to find out why the anomaly happened and how to prevent it from happening again.

About the Author

R. C. Seely started the Americanus Libertae in the winter 2012. It started with a blog at Wordpress.com with that name. That same time he wrote the book 'We the Rodents.'

He started Mojo Publishing at that time and a YouTube channel.

He continues the efforts of Americanus Libertae of exposing the dangers in Pop Culture.

He can be reached at americanuslibertae@gmail.com and releases updates at RCSeely@twitter.com.

ALSO BY THIS R. C. SEELY